KINGDOM RACE THEOLOGY

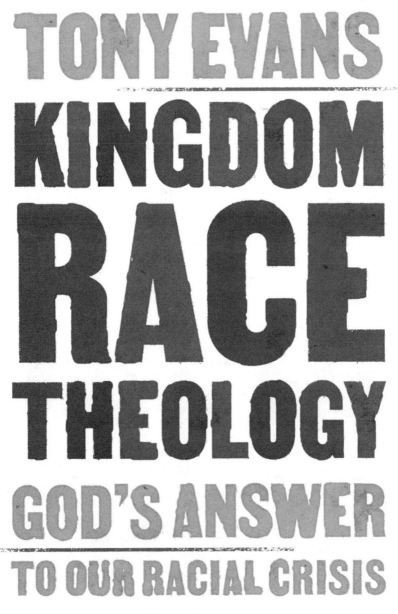

TONY EVANS

KINGDOM RACE THEOLOGY

GOD'S ANSWER

TO OUR RACIAL CRISIS

MOODY PUBLISHERS
CHICAGO

Adapted from chapters 10, 12, 15, and 16 of *Oneness Embraced: Kingdom Race Theology for Reconciliation, Unity, and Justice* by Tony Evans, © 2011, 2022. A portion of chapter 4 was first published as "A Kingdom Strategy for Community Transformation," *The Urban Alternative*, 2020. Some of the material in chapter 4 was first published in the *Dallas Morning News*. Used by permission.

Scripture quotations taken from the (NASB®) New American Standard Bible®, Copyright © 1960, 1971, 1977, 1995 by The Lockman Foundation. Used by permission. All rights reserved. www.lockman.org

Edited by Kevin Mungons
Interior Design: Ragont Design
Cover Design: Erik M. Peterson

Library of Congress Cataloging-in-Publication Data

Names: Evans, Tony, 1949- author.
Title: Kingdom race theology : God's answer to our racial crisis / Tony
   Evans.
Description: Chicago : Moody Publishers, [2022] | Includes bibliographical
   references. | Summary: "America's racial conflict isn't over-and the
   current discussion hasn't brought us any closer. The beginnings of a
   helpful dialogue on diversity became a heated battle about systemic
   racism, white privilege, and Critical Race Theory, all framed by the
   slogan "black lives matter." Bestselling author Tony Evans answers with
   a fearless and prophetic voice, pointing to God's Word as the only
   lasting solution. Kingdom Race Theology helps people and churches commit
   to restitution, reconciliation, and responsibility. Together we can work
   across racial lines to repair the damage done by a long history of
   racial injustice"-- Provided by publisher.
Identifiers: LCCN 2021044627 (print) | LCCN 2021044628 (ebook) | ISBN
   9780802429193 (paperback) | ISBN 9780802473899 (ebook)
Subjects: LCSH: Race relations--Religious aspects--Christianity. |
   Racism--Religious aspects--Christianity. | United States--Race
   relations. | Racism--United States. | BISAC: RELIGION / Christian Living
   / Social Issues | RELIGION / Christian Living / Spiritual Growth
Classification: LCC BT734.2 .E929 2022 (print) | LCC BT734.2 (ebook) |
   DDC 277.308/3--dc23
LC record available at https://lccn.loc.gov/2021044627
LC ebook record available at https://lccn.loc.gov/2021044628

Originally delivered by fleets of horse-drawn wagons, the affordable paperbacks from D. L. Moody's publishing house resourced the church and served everyday people. Now, after more than 125 years of publishing and ministry, Moody Publishers' mission remains the same—even if our delivery systems have changed a bit. For more information on other books (and resources) created from a biblical perspective, go to www.moodypublishers.com or write to:

Moody Publishers
820 N. LaSalle Boulevard
Chicago, IL 60610

1 3 5 7 9 10 8 6 4 2

Printed in the United States of America

CONTENTS

Introduction: Why This Book   7

1. The Need for Kingdom Race Theology   13

2. The Meaning of Kingdom Race Theology   39

3. The Focus of Kingdom Race Theology   69

4. The Practice of Kingdom Race Theology   89

    Appendix: The Urban Alternative   107

    Acknowledgments   117

    Notes   119

INTRODUCTION: WHY THIS BOOK

We are living in a time of racial chaos, confusion, and conflict. The painful history of our country's racial divide continues to plague us as a contemporary reality with no apparent resolution in sight.

We, the church, have allowed these battles to divide people of faith even more deeply than before, making us a co-conspirator to the racial epidemic we are continuing to experience in our nation. We cannot afford this. Our nation cannot afford this. Our sons and daughters—whether black, white, or any other color—cannot afford this. We can no longer afford to sit idly by representing the body of Christ as a "mere wreck" of its divine design. The solutions to the issues we face today are found only by applying a biblical and divine standard as answers to the questions before us. The church should be a model, at such a time as this, to reveal to the world what true oneness, equality, justice, and freedom can produce. Hell advances on the church's doorsteps with fervent speed, and as long as we remain divided, it will continue to do so.

We can resist hell's advances and heal a broken nation if we are willing to come together. First we must fill in our own gaps of understanding, our knowledge of our unique histories, and our relationships. We can repair our own fissures that lead to even greater divides. Then we will have visible solutions we can offer to a frayed society.

This short book introduces some of the material I cover in *Oneness Embraced: A Kingdom Race Theology for Reconciliation, Unity and Justice.* For those who are interested in a full treatment of this subject and its history in the church, by all means read the longer book. This shorter book also contains material I presented at Oak Cliff Bible Fellowship in Dallas. As I addressed these issues at my own church, I found myself drawn into the national debate over race, racism, justice, and social theories. Sometimes I found my position mischaracterized by those who claimed I endorsed their views of the issue.[1]

Like all other ideologies, racial theories must be examined and critiqued based on their conformity to God's Word. Race and racism cannot be the grid for determining theology. Rather, Scripture alone must be the final arbitrator of what is legitimate or illegitimate for this and every other social theory.

Though my response to racial and social theories affirms the sufficiency and authority of Scripture over all ideologies, I do not declare them null and void of any merit. I may disagree, for example, with popular interpretations of racial themes or the connections many of their followers make to anti-theistic ideologies. I do not disagree with the totality of the points or purposes as they were originally intended—especially its teaching of a more holistic and accurate history through narrative and creative storytelling. A proper understanding and application of God's Word will enable us to nuance and distinguish between that which is valid or invalid (Heb. 4:12). It will also enable us to identify and correct the misuse of religion and the Bible by those who illegitimately use it to maintain racial superiority, division, and privilege.

One of the challenges of contemporary social theories is that many of their iterations have gained a popular foothold, forever locking black/white relations in an oppressor/oppressed matrix. To teach or imply to a young child that he or she will always be oppressed is to instill a victim mentality into that child's worldview and, thus, limit that child's ability to pursue his or her full potential. By focusing so heavily on institutional structures and systems, it often reduces personal responsibility, allowances for righting wrongs, or individual changes of mindset. Conversely, to imply that skin color and their concomitant privileges automatically places a person in an oppressor grouping locks them into a status from which there is no meaningful exit. Also, social theories that give academic analysis but leave us void of practical solutions create an unsatisfied hunger that leaves us stuck in a never-ending cycle of analysis without resolution.

How do we balance these ideas? It is my contention that the core of the racial disunity problem stems from a failure to understand and execute a kingdom-based theology on both righteousness and justice. A balance between the two is absolutely critical since it is from God's kingdom throne that both righteousness and justice originate. "Righteousness and justice are the foundation of Your throne; lovingkindness and truth go before You" (Ps. 89:14).

The balance between righteousness and justice is so crucial that God's commitment to bring His kingdom benefits to bear on one generation is tied to training the next generation in how to function effectively with it (Gen. 18:19). When either side, righteousness or justice, is missed or reduced in significance, then the individual, family, church, and society will be out of balance.

INTRODUCING KINGDOM RACE THEOLOGY

As a biblical *kingdomologist*, I am unashamedly committed to the absolute authority and inerrancy of Scripture as my final source of truth (John 17:17). As a black man, I am proud of the unique history and culture God has allowed me to partake of, as well as the unique perspective they give me. As an American, I am committed to this nation of my birth, along with the freedom and opportunities it offers and the oneness it seeks to achieve. It is my goal in this work and in my ministry to provide and promote a kingdom approach to the subject of the church, race, justice, and oneness. I seek to take the issues out of the realm of human speculation and esoteric analysis as well as the limitation of the kingdom of men and place them squarely in the hands of the kingdom of God, which is where they belong.

Our racial divide is a sinful disease. Over-the-counter human remedies won't fix it; they merely mask the symptoms for a season. What we need is a prescription from the Creator to destroy this cancer before it destroys us. What the church desperately needs is a Kingdom Race Theology (KRT) that gives a biblical framework and practical solutions to our ongoing ethnic divide. This book is my humble attempt to provide such an ecclesiological framework. If the church can ever get this issue of oneness right, then we can help America finally become the "one nation under God" that we declare ourselves to be. When we get it right in the church house—first—then we can spread it to the White House and beyond (Eph. 3:10).

kingdom agenda: the visible manifestation of the comprehensive rule of God.

Scripture is clear that the spiritual condition of God's people greatly affects whether there is order or chaos in society (2 Chron. 15:3–6). Kingdom Race Theology is part of a broader theological framework and worldview that I call the *Kingdom Agenda* (see my book of the same title for a comprehensive review of this worldview). In short, the "Kingdom Agenda" is the visible manifestation of the comprehensive rule of God over every area of life. God's kingdom has clearly addressed the issue of race and racism. He has spoken on this subject and has not stuttered. It is my humble goal in this book to give a biblical, theological, and practical analysis of the issues along with an individual and collective action plan for resolving this stain on the church and our nation.

We'll begin to explore this subject by looking at the need for Kingdom Race Theology and the importance of defining the terms we use when we talk about the issue of race.

1

THE NEED FOR KINGDOM RACE THEOLOGY

On May 25, 2020, the racial conflict in America rose to a whole new level with the very public murder of George Floyd. His death, brought about by a white police officer kneeling on his neck, was filmed on a cellphone for the world to see. Like fireworks exploding on the Fourth of July, this watershed event ignited a racial firestorm throughout America and beyond. Floyd's death was the proverbial straw that broke the camel's back as black, white, and brown people took to the streets in protest. The tragedy provoked lament and grief over a past whose effects, both covert and overt, are yet to be addressed or healed. It also brought to the forefront a number of contemporary social movements and theories that sought to address the matter of racism and injustice. You may be familiar with these social movements and I'll go into greater detail on each of them in my expanded revision of *Oneness Embraced*, but in short, I'll give a brief overview as we start out:

BLACK LIVES MATTER

> **Critical Race Theory:**
>
> a post-civil rights social theory that demonstrates how unjust laws have served as the embedded foundation and filter through which racist attitudes, behavior, policies, and structures have been rooted.

The focus and support of the mantra *Black Lives Matter* is legitimately born out of tragedy. It originally came to a more formalized structure in 2013 and rose on the national scene after the events of Ferguson, Missouri, and Michael Brown's death.[1] It rose to global prominence after the death of George Floyd. The movement highlights the injustices against black lives in much the same way that white evangelicals emphasize that the lives of unborn babies matter.

The Black Lives Matter movement essentially has two aspects. There is the informal movement by those who stand up for injustice against black lives, using peaceful protests and education to bring about healthy cultural and police reforms. There is also the official organization, trademarked as Black Lives Matter, and founded by Patrisse Cullors (who has since resigned amid controversy), Alicia Garza, and Opal Tometi. The formal entity of Black Lives Matter advocates key elements of an agenda that cannot be supported by serious Christians. It rejects the primacy and protection of the nuclear family while promoting the acceptance of gay and transgender lifestyles.[2] In addition, the founders openly embrace an ideological framework of Marxism, an anti-theistic movement.[3] The Black Lives Matter focus has merit in the overarching mission of social injustice for black lives in particular, an oft-overlooked aspect of social reform. But like all social movements, Black Lives Matter must be examined, analyzed, and critiqued against the backdrop of God's inerrant Word.

CRITICAL RACE THEORY

In the wake of the collective upheaval taking place, the Black Lives Matter movement also gave fresh legs to Critical Race Theory, which now stands tall at the core of today's racial debate.

Critical Race Theory may be defined as *a post-civil rights social theory that demonstrates how unjust laws have served as the embedded foundation and filter through which racist attitudes, behavior, policies, and structures have been rooted and continue to influence the fabric of American life, politics, and systems, even after those laws were changed.*

CRT proponents view race as a social construct created to expand or protect power and control. It also holds that the foundation of society's institutions and power structures are based on white privilege. Proponents frequently contend that these institutions and structures are inherently racist in that they are consciously or subconsciously used to maintain and expand the economic and political power of white people at the expense of people of color.[4] Proponents of CRT also contend that storytelling and narrative-based knowledge is a leading element in changing cultures, affecting worldviews, and even addressing systemic issues. One of the leading CRT theorists, Kimberlé Crenshaw, defines it as "a way of looking at law's role platforming, facilitating, producing, and even insulating racial inequality in our country."[5]

Never has there been a more volatile subject separating schools, school boards, churches, denominations, organizations, businesses and even personal relationships through heated emotions and often verbal vitriol.

THE 1619 PROJECT

Using the framework of CRT, the 1619 Project was created in August 2019 by Nikole Hannah-Jones with contributors from the *New York Times* and the *New York Times Magazine*. The journalism project argues that the very existence and establishment of America was rooted in the purpose of protecting the institution of slavery that they say began, not in 1776, but in 1619 with the first group of slaves arriving in Jamestown, Virginia. While the year of the first slaves to arrive in America is debatable (some placing it as far back as the early 1500s and some arguing that the individuals in 1619 were indentured servants), the issue of dates isn't the most alarming. The 1619 Project contends, among other historically inaccurate statements, that the American Revolution was fought in order to preserve the institution of slavery, a glaringly wrong conclusion that has brought it a tremendous amount of intellectual criticism.[6] Many historians have criticized its historical validity in other areas as well.

1776 UNITES

A number of black ministers and civic leaders have joined together to create the black-led movement called *1776 Unites* that served as a rebuttal to the 1619 Project. In the dedication of the book of essays published as a response to the 1619 Project, originator Robert Woodson writes,

No nation is perfect, but America—more than any other—is a place where people from every imaginable background have been able to pursue their dreams and realize their potential. . . . This is as true of black Americans as it is anyone else. During the worst of Jim Crow, we built thriving communities full of families, churches, businesses, and countless civic institutions. On the very soil where we once toiled in forced labor, we found the seeds of our liberation. At a time when many are trying to pull us apart by stoking grievances and sowing discord, the overwhelming majority of Americans remain devoted to our founding principles and to one another.[7]

This increased focus on racial issues comes with new tensions. This short book is not intended to go into depth on these movements but to focus more on the solution I am calling Kingdom Race Theology.

Regardless of the many movements at hand, the many definitions given to certain terms is also contributing to our cultural confusion. It seems that everyone has a different way of interpreting what terms mean at this time. Certain terms such as *systemic racism, white privilege, microaggression, implicit bias, victimization,* and others trigger emotional responses that often kick opportunities for authentic conversations to the curb. A mixed bag of personal definitions of these terms combined with a variety of personal experiences have turned the dialogue on diversity into a heated battle of hearts, oftentimes leading only to confusion. This has caused many on both sides to throw the proverbial "baby out with the bath water." As a result, people reject these concepts, ideologies, and viewpoints out of hand rather than pursuing an honest intellectual exchange on what may be valuable.

The redefinition of terms and multiple meanings of words, often dependent on who is using them, has made it almost impossible to discuss relevant issues reasonably. As Thomas Sowell puts it, "One of the many signs of verbal virtuosity among intellectuals is the repackaging of words to mean things that are not only different from, but sometimes the direct opposite of, their original meanings."[8] Thus, before we start any discussion on racism and reconciliation, I want to start by giving you my definitions for what I'm about to address.

> **racism:**
>
> the conscious or unconscious belief in the superiority of one race over another race, or ethnicities, which manifests itself in a variety of dismissive, oppressive, or exploitive ways.

RACISM AND SYSTEMIC RACISM

Many people define racism in many different ways. This is due to the tremendous variety in both the practical and emotive experiences that form the perspectives through which life is viewed. I define racism as *the conscious or unconscious belief in the superiority of one race over another race, or ethnicities, which manifests itself in a variety of dismissive, oppressive, or exploitive ways*. Racism shows up in the use of power, influence, resources, or communication, which is employed to discriminate against, marginalize, exploit and/or subjugate people of another race or ethnicity. When unaddressed prejudice gets married to power there is going to be an unintended pregnancy that will give birth to the evil of racism.

I have heard the assertion, as I'm sure you have, that "systemic racism" no longer exists. I often hear that from people who with their next breath say they are not racist, and some might even add that they never owned slaves. These two statements are often tied so closely that they appear to be a defensive posture. By negating the existence of systemic racism or its consequences, they attempt to absolve any personal feelings of attachment to it. The white author Ken Wytsma connects this defensiveness to a need for personal comfort. After being told to not use the term *white privilege* in a talk at a Christian university, he observed that "our desire for comfort leads us to defensiveness when we are confronted with questions of race." He continues with a good question: "But when did our comfort become the driving value?"[9]

Yet I have also heard the same denial of systemic racism by many well-known black scholars and conservative black theologians, who do so with a focus on personal responsibility and moral values. They seem hesitant to acknowledge the existence or lingering corporate, social, political, and economic effects of racism, as if this somehow eliminates the possibility and primacy of promoting personal responsibilities.

And while I agree that our laws and legal systems on paper have been addressed and corrected over the years, I would assert that certain cultural repercussions remain. Just as a football team may win or lose on paper but perform very differently in the actual game, paper laws intended to help don't always produce equitable outcomes. This is because the carrying out of those laws, as well as the residual effects of the earlier laws, applies to people, not paper. Whenever you insert humanity into the equation, you've inserted sin and sin, invariably, messes things up.

Systemic racism, or the resultant lingering effects of it, continues to show up in pockets and places across our land. You see it in unequal access to quality health care and lack of affordable nutritious meal options in urban centers. This leads to increased obesity and negative health outcomes (physical and mental), as well as lower access to quality job opportunities. It also leads to the disparate amount of transferable generational wealth largely due to the equally disparate numbers of home ownership over the last century.

It can also be argued that systemic racism exists through less overt, but cyclically produced ramifications of decades of racist-based legislations (again, whether or not these legislations still exist). Urban crowding and its lasting legacy of poor education, dismantled families, and high crime is one example. There is no "law" keeping black Americans living in highly populated urban centers, but there is also not much of a way out since many of the individuals there face so many hardships at such a young age, coupled with inadequate training, which often prevents upward mobility.

systemic racism:

racist practices and processes embedded in and shaping the social, political, economic, legal, educational, religious, infrastructural, and medical systems and policies of a society— initially established and perpetuated by the government.

It is my belief that racism has embedded itself not only in many individual hearts throughout our history but also, to varying degrees, in the many structures of our society. Whether those structures are political, economic, legal or many others, they impact how entire groups of people think and live.

Systemic racism is said to exist whenever racism has become part of the policies, procedures, and mindset by which a particular entity or societal structure operates. And while law-based existences of systemic racism may have been overturned or done away with through nationwide reforms, the lasting implications of many of these systems can still be felt by many. Some people get stuck in semantics over whether or not officially sanctioned "systemic racism" exists in our nation through governmental laws, or whether it exists through cyclical and cultural effects. Instead, believers ought to be open to examining real life struggles and how to solve them.

Systemic racism recognizes that the sin of racism is, or was, not only a personal issue, but a corporate one as well. In fact, systemic racism even recognizes that while individuals themselves might not be racist, the structures and entities in which these individuals live or function can be established and still run on racist policies, practices, ideals, and intentions. I have heard many people argue against systemic racism through arguing that not all people of a certain race are racist. But that is not what systemic racism is. To acknowledge that systemic racism exists is not the same thing as declaring all white people to be racist. Systemic racism speaks to the structures, policies, and institutions of a society and not to the entirety of the individuals who inhabit it.

Thus, I define systemic racism as *the presence, or cyclical resultant effects, of racist practices and processes embedded in and shaping the social, political, economic, legal, educational, religious, infrastructural, and medical systems and policies of a society—initially established and perpetuated by the government.* These then overlap and interconnect in such a way as to give an unjust advantage of resources, rights, mindsets, and privilege for a majority number of one race while denying, or limiting, it to a majority number of other races or ethnicities. Systemic racism's impact over the decades when it loomed large still impacts a myriad of things such as employment, education, housing, incarceration, health care, family dynamics, wealth gaps, and much more. Whatever the system or structure of racist realities (known or unknown), these contribute overall to inequitable opportunities for personal advancement or personal wholeness. These same principles can apply to class divisions or caste systems and have existed in other nations divided by ethnic or racial constructs. It is not only a white/black matrix, depending on the nation and the group in power.

Theological comparison

Perhaps a theological comparison can help illustrate the point. Men are born under the evil law of sin and death. This sentences all mankind to the slavery and oppression of sin (Rom. 8:2; Eph. 2:1–3). Upon conversion, that law is cancelled and replaced with a new law, the law of the spirit (Rom. 6:6). This new law legally frees believers from the law of sin and death. However, just because the law changed, the abiding struggle with sin did not automatically disappear (Rom. 7:14–25). Only consistent growth in the application of the law of the spirit can overcome the flesh's attempt to keep us functioning as spiritual slaves (Gal. 5:16–18). Failure to apply the new law means that the abiding effects of the evil system of the old law continues due to the historical power of the old laws' influence on our flesh, even though it has been replaced. This reality serves to deny believers the full experience of freedom the new law promises (Rom. 8:3–13; Gal. 5:13). Likewise, the abiding effects of racism continue at various levels depending on the willingness of people to submit to the new laws of justice that have been established.

Historical comparison

Our shared history begins with the system of whites enslaving blacks, which arguably began as far back as the 1500s. Of course we are all aware of the evil system of slavery, a legal system enacted to oppress black people based on the color of our skin. But what many people do not realize is that when slavery was dissolved, the ideologies within it merely got embedded into other structures in society. So while the practice of slavery was outlawed, the principles that undergirded it remained present through other legalized systems from the Black Codes to Jim Crow. Thus, when people point to slavery as a contributing factor to present-day issues, they are pointing to slavery and the resultant practices and policies that flowed out of it up until now.

For example, after slavery there immediately developed a practice called debt servitude (peonage), where an employer would compel an individual to work in order to pay off a debt. This was primarily used by landowners or merchant suppliers as a way of keeping blacks in a state of perpetual servanthood. On the surface, debt servitude does not necessarily seem evil. It is only when you uncover the ways in which it was enacted upon minority ethnicities after slavery that you see the evil for what it was. Price gouging on life-sustaining items such as flour, eggs, or milk, in order to create lifelong dependence and debt, was commonplace. And while this form of peonage was outlawed by Congress in 1867 due to its imbedded evils, many people found a way to continue the principles of the practice through other means.

In addition to debt servitude, the criminal justice system sought to exploit a clause in the Thirteenth Amendment that stated a person was free unless they were a criminal. This resulted in an extension of peonage well into the 1900s, through the profitable practice of convict leasing.

What this clause unleashed was an avalanche of criminal charges against black boys and men for even the most minor of infractions. Often no crime was committed at all, or it was invented, such as an accusation of littering with no proof, or planted proof. For example, certain vagrancy laws even made it a crime to be unemployed at a very young age.

Once put in prison, these young boys and men would frequently be held way beyond what they were arrested for, and forced to live and work in conditions that in many cases were worse than the conditions in slavery. From a purely a business standpoint, the well-being and the health condition of the slave mattered more to the master than to the prison owner. If prisoners were lost to death or disease, they could be replaced with another criminal without much effort. The prison owner also had no long-term view of the life and long-term contribution of the convict to seek to preserve. Thus, conditions deteriorated rapidly as people learned how to work, and fill, the system. For example, "In the first two years that Alabama leased its prisoners, nearly 20 percent of them died. In the following year, mortality rose to 35 percent. In the fourth, nearly 45 percent were killed."[10]

The *New York Times* gives insight into why so many died when it described the condition of these prisons in December 1882. It "told of black prisoners packed into a single cramped cabin like slaves on the Atlantic passage. The building had no windows. Vermin-ridden bunks stacked three high were covered with straw and 'ravaged blankets.' 'Revoltingly filthy' food was served cold from unwashed coal buckets, and all 150 black convicts shared three half-barrel tubs for washing."[11]

As you can imagine, many black families had their strongest male contributors plucked from their homes at a young age during the decades of convict leasing. Convict leasing was a lucrative practice to produce goods at a low cost. The price of using criminals for work assignments was less than a fraction of a penny. For instance, in 1866, Texas leased 250 men to two railroads for $12.50 a month.[12] A dollar could buy the labor of twenty black prisoners for a full month.

Not only did these systemically racist policies increase the wealth and opportunities for powerful whites in America (a generational wealth handed down through inheritances, which still contributes to the wealth gap today), but the policies also dismantled the nucleus of the black family by removing a large percentage of black males from homes. This strategy by those in power (i.e., that of dismantling the nucleus of the black family) has continued over the centuries through a variety of approaches. As believers in the Word of God, we know that Satan's primary way to keep a people group subjugated or in a perpetual state of cyclical self-sabotage is to attack, and destroy, the family unit. Satan is not above using sinful people and broken systems to carry out his agenda.

Many point to the war on drugs and the war on crime and other policies created in the late 1960s and early 1970s as an intentional response to thwart the gains achieved through the Civil Rights movement and a strategic extension of this targeted attack to dismantle the nuclear black family. In fact, although less easy to see, the outcomes of the policies left many calling it the "new Jim Crow." As Stanford Law School graduate Michelle Alexander writes, "No other country in the world imprisons so many of its racial or ethnic minorities. The United States imprisons a larger percentage of its black population than South Africa did at the height of the apartheid. . . . These stark racial disparities cannot be explained by rates of drug crime."[13]

But in addition to its root, peonage, and before the new Jim Crow, systemic racism showed up as our nation grew in numbers through the way people were denied employment or educational opportunities during the actual era of the Jim Crow segregation. Jim Crow laws of the South were the official standards that inculcated and established that one group would be allowed to benefit while another group would be disenfranchised. It also showed up in churches that were unwilling to accept people of a different race, or theological institutions that were unwilling to train people of a different race.

My experiences with racism

Systemic racism impacted me personally in a number of ways. When I tried to enter the media ministry in my mid 30s, I was turned down by every station I sought to get on, except for one in Houston. Some would even go as far as to tell me that a black speaker would offend too many of their white listeners. While there was no law stating a black preacher couldn't air his sermons on white-owned radio stations, there was an embedded cultural system in place denying black preachers equal opportunity and equal access for upward mobility.

Now does that mean every radio station listener was racist and would have been offended at that time? No. Did I think every white person was racist at that time because I couldn't get on radio stations to broadcast my sermons? No again. That's because the existence of systemic racism, or its cyclical outworkings, does not mean that every white person in America is racist. But it did mean that the system of Christian radio in the early 1980s and before functioned, to some degree, with unwritten yet very clearly racist processes, standards, and assumptions.

I have plenty of personal illustrations where I have faced systemic racism. One took place when I was asked to go speak to a group of Christian golfers at a golf club. Those who invited me wanted me to teach the Bible in order to make a spiritual impact on the members. I went, but after I got there I discovered that I was visiting a place that I could not join. I was welcome as a preacher but not as a person.

Not too long ago, the church where I pastor purchased the golf course adjacent to our church, 155 acres of prime acres in the southwest section of Oak Cliff. I did not propose buying the course because I like golf—in fact, I don't even play. I wanted us to purchase it in order to have a say in what happens in our community. We own several hundred acres of land in this area for that very purpose—to invest in the well-being and maintenance of our urban community.

The interesting history about the golf course was that black people could not play on it until the 1990s. This is because blacks were not allowed to be members when it was built in the 1950s.

Now when the golf course turned into a member-owned course some years later, there was no longer a law that kept black people from joining. The law got removed because our culture was changing and that kind of law was no longer viewed as acceptable. But even though the unjust law had been removed, the system was still plagued with racism. For example, before a person could become a member, an existing member had to recommend you. That shouldn't be much of a problem until you find out that after you are recommended, two-thirds of the membership had to also vote for you.

So let's say a white man recommends a black man to join the golf club. They are going up against a system that states that two-thirds of his peers have to agree with the way he is thinking, which is why no black man was voted in until 1994. Not because there was a law against it. There wasn't. But there was a system in place that operated on racist principles.

But taking this further—let's say as a white man you are part of the one-third who voted to have the black man admitted to join. Or you are the white man who proposed he join. Well, you still lost because of the two-thirds who were the majority in the system. Now, you could argue that you are not part of the two-thirds and are not like those people. You could also argue that you are not a racist, and you could be absolutely right. But the point is that the system you were a part of was racist. Acknowledging the existence of systemic racism is not the same as saying that all white people are racist. But denying its existence out of a spirit of defensiveness or an honest lack of personal involvement is insensitive to the plight of the many impacted by it either in the past or present.

> Wherever systemic racism exists, or whatever you choose to label it, there are real issues plaguing millions of Americans today.

While there are varying views on the degrees to which systemic racism is reflected in our lives today, one thing is clear: wherever systemic racism (or its repercussions) exists, or whatever you choose to label it, there are real issues plaguing millions of Americans today. And much of this shows up in affecting primarily lower-class black Americans (and certainly other subgroups and class groups). Rather than spend all of our time arguing semantics or trying to pin blame (or deflect it), we as Christ followers ought to acknowledge the issues at hand and righteously address them.

A person merely needs to walk through the urban center of Baltimore, where I grew up, to witness the inadequate facilities for equal educational opportunities for Baltimore's minorities, as compared with the educational systems in the suburbs. And while admittedly there have been opportunities to address these issues by electing minority leadership, there has been an obvious failure to take advantage of those positions to bring about a greater good for the community at large. Historic systemic corruption can become so deeply imbedded that it can show up even in those who you would think would want to change it.

As recently as 2020, graduation rates in the urban areas of Maryland were only 69.9 percent while the average rate for the entire state is much higher at 86.7 percent.[14] Not only that, graduation requirements have been so grossly lowered in the urban schools that the Baltimore City Community College reported that 93 percent of all incoming students (70 percent of whom come from Baltimore's city-schools) required remedial classes.[15] Lowering standards does not prepare an individual for success. In fact, it often sets them up for induced failure. This contributes to a lowering of their own personal esteem through the concept of mismatched placement, which can then be handed down generationally, according to famed black economist Thomas Sowell.[16]

Systemic racism and political ideology

Systemic racism isn't a politically-neutral-perpetuated issue either, as both sides often like to believe. Both sides of the aisle have contributed to its generational mess. In fact, much of it has been produced most recently through what people have labeled liberal progressive legislation and policies, beginning in the mid 1960s with the war on

poverty. Any policy that seeks to strip individual responsibility, ambition, and values from people, or dismantles
the primacy of the nuclear family does more harm than
good. Systemic racism camouflaged as charity is another
insidious form of injustice.

In fact, compare the statistics of racial income gaps
prior to the war on poverty and other civil rights legislation and after it. The income gap has remained the same,
if not worsened in some areas.[17] Liberal policies, along
with an errant view of the legitimate divinely created
scope of civil government, fall short in producing the
outcomes that the liberals claim they will. Rather, the
policies produce an unhealthy and illegitimate depen-
dency on government.

Shelby Steele describes this conundrum between
liberal ideology and outcome as the "great internal contradiction of white liberalism: that its paternalism, its
focus on whites rather than on blacks as the agents of
change, allows white supremacy to slip in the back door
and once again define the fundamental relationship between whites and blacks . . . Whites are agents; blacks
are agented."[18]

Systemic racism, or its ensuing effects, often comes
stacked over a lifetime, but it can also be viewed like
dominos standing on a table. If you knock one domino
over, the rest will likely fall. Children and youth need
opportunities to excel in education, starting with a
strong nuclear family, strong church, limited exposure to

damaging influences, strong role models, healthy food and life balances, character development and behavioral accountability, and an accurate view of personal potential. Without this foundation, their opportunities for social and vocational successes diminish later in life as well. One thing leads to another. And this then is passed down generationally as poor life choices lead to generational consequences stacked on each other in what can appear to outsiders as communal self-sabotage. The net result is that hopelessness rules.

Systemic racism and education

The refusal to offer parents school choice (where the funding follows the kids and not vice versa) greatly disadvantages the opportunity and progress for the disenfranchised, locking them into an inefficient educational monopoly that underserves them. From a kingdom perspective, education starts with the family not with the state. Such competition in the marketplace will inevitably lead to improved educational opportunity for those who need it most.

Education is merely one domino on the table that enacts separate standards based on color and class. When a person is faced with several realities of systemic racism in his or her life (this is referred to as *intersectionality*), along with an often-generalized and dismissive stance by the culture at large on whether or not he or she faces any inequitable hardships at all, he or she confronts an emotional, psychological, and practical barrier toward personal growth and development. Sometimes, and far too often, paralyzingly so. This creates a self-imposed prophecy of living up to the lowered expectations offered through permissive policies.

OUR RESPONSIBILITY

While an individual today may not be personally racist, they can contribute to the racist structures by supporting the inequitable systems still in place, or by denying that they exist. If you are nonracist yourself but do not actively oppose racism (willing to speak or work against racism and racist systems where they show up), you are failing to fulfill the whole letter of the law of love (Rom. 13:8). As we saw earlier, sin is not just a bad behavior you do but rather sin is also knowing something good to do, and choosing not to do it (James 4:17; Isa. 58).

Yes, sin is personal. Far too many people argue that racism is not something to be addressed by the church because the church should focus on personal sins only. But Nehemiah 1:6–7 coupled with Daniel 9:4–6 links our personal sins to the collective group, and to the systems upon which culture is founded and runs.

Think of a sprint where some racers are allowed to start earlier or are allowed to start at a point much ahead of another group. The other group spends their whole time just trying to catch up—the sprint is intrinsically not equitable. This illustration may help you develop more empathy for this historical reality of systemic racism. When you can grasp this reality, how frequently it appears in our culture, and its resultant cyclical effects, you can gain sensitivity to the conversations at hand or legitimate protests taking place. Again, the existence of racism cannot and must not be used as a reason for rejecting personal and corporate responsibility, even as injustice is being properly addressed. It should also be noted that while righteous protesting is biblically based (Acts 16:35–40), rioting is not (Rom. 3:14–18). Rioting must never be accepted as a righteous way of redress.

Despite all of our forward progress, there still remains within our society certain critical elements that need to be corrected, adjusted, or even entirely revamped so that equal opportunity toward emotional, physical, and psychological health as well as personal development in education and skills training is granted to all people, irrespective of race. I have seen a tremendous increase in virtue-signaling and social media posting about racial unity over the last few years but what I have not seen much at all is any real changes in the true racial integration of relationships, Christian organizations' staff or church makeup, or even personal investment in addressing the broken systems that continue to plague pockets of our land. Reading a book is great. Posting about it online gets the word out. Also, good. But when you close this book, seek to do something to make a difference for good

in the world in which we live. This difference should be
led by the church publicly operating with a Kingdom
Race Theology, not a culturally determined sociology.

Contemporary social movements and theories must
be examined, analyzed, and critiqued against the backdrop of God's inerrant Word. While I contend that some
of the observations and approaches of contemporary
social theories are rooted in historical analysis as they
seek to address the insidious racism carried out through
overt and covert words and actions, as well as the in-
effective policies enacted under the banner of "colorblind" laws of the past and present, the foundation of
these social theories is wrong. I say that the foundation
is wrong because the grid on which it exists is founded
on a sociological perspective rather than a theologically
sound and biblically based kingdom agenda worldview.
While racism is an evil sin severely condemned by God,
it is neither the first sin, the only sin, nor the defining
classification of sin. Idolatry, which is always rooted in
pride, is the superintending sin in Scripture. Racism is
certainly one major humanistic evil expression of the sin
of idolatry since it is an attack on the value of the image
of God in which all mankind of every ethnicity is created. When the idolatrous sin of racism is properly and
comprehensively addressed by the church and is accom-
panied by the practice of biblical unity, then we can offer
the culture more than pious rhetoric but also visible solutions. This is the goal of Kingdom Race Theology.

THE MEANING OF KINGDOM RACE THEOLOGY

America continues to grapple with the unresolved, sinful, evil diseases of racism, culturalism, and classism. The sickness is too deep for over-the-counter remedies. Any pandemic that lasts this long and runs this deep won't be solved by a trip to your local drugstore. Radical surgery is needed.

Many contemporary social movements call for racial justice. These movements give legitimate insights into some of the key areas that cannot be ignored if we are to address the problems of race and racism in our country. They fall short, however, in effectively addressing the spiritual cause and cure for this ongoing social malaise. This is because sociology that is not firmly rooted in proper theology will always fall short of fully evaluating and resolving the effects of sin in society that leads to

injustice. Socialism in the name of equity, the redistribution of wealth, and compassion operate from a collectivistic worldview where civil government, to varying
degrees, becomes the major means of either controlling,
owning, or administrating the ways and means of pro-
duction and the distribution of goods and services. Such
a position illegitimately inverts God's limited purpose for
civil government, which is to maintain a safe, just, righteous, and compassionately responsible environment and
to free the marketplace from tyranny so that freedom can
flourish—starting with the individual. Scripture is clear
that the centralized governmental control of trade is the
economic system of the Antichrist (Rev. 13:16–17).

On the other hand, capitalism is an economic system
based on the free market, limited government, personal
productivity and prosperity. But this system often opens
up the door to the sin of greed and exploitation in the
name of profit. Slavery is an example of this, but the
exploitation of the working class in a capitalist society is
not limited to extremes such as slavery. These exploita-
tions take place at a multiplicity of levels in our contemporary culture.

People are looking to a system to solve things today,
but no system has truly solved the injustices in society
because no system (capitalism, socialism, or any other)
is free from the human imprint of sin. Without the sinful
hearts of mankind being addressed, all political and economic systems will fall short of effectively addressing

the injustices they wish to resolve. This is why righteous and just laws, enforced by civil government, are necessary to restrict the evil activity of sinful people (Rom. 13:1–7; 1 Tim. 1:8–10).

To address the chaotic racial confusion in our culture we need something much more effective, something that will not only address systemic issues but also the root of these systemic issues—sin. So as clearly as I know how, I would like this chapter to address as specifically as possible this issue of race, culture, and class that has been muddied by a million different voices. I'm offering a theological, kingdom-based approach to the issues of racism and injustices. As I've taught it, kingdomology is *the theological framework and belief system that asserts that God's purpose in history in the manifestation of His glory through the establishment and advancement of His eternal kingdom on earth.* Kingdomology views this purpose as the unifying theme of Scripture. This purpose is accomplished progressively in history through human instrumentality, over and against demonic and human opposition, as mankind functions in covenant with God.

Today we have voices making claims about *which* life matters. Or whose life matters *more*. Bear in mind, all human life is created in the image of God. Therefore, all lives matter.

However, underneath the banner that God has created all people in His image, there are inequities that must be addressed. For example, the life of the unborn matters. And thus there is an emphasis on justice for the life of the unborn. Few Bible-believing people question this emphasis. Many believe that injustice in the womb must be under the umbrella that the fetus is a human life, and since all life matters, that unborn life matters.

Now to emphasize that black lives matter is also a subset under the banner that all life matters. To say that black lives matter is not to say that other lives do not matter. It is to emphasize an injustice carried out over time toward a particular group of people. The problems of these various approaches arise once you extract any specific scenario and remove it from the umbrella of God's creation. You then create your own independent cause.

There is no discussion of sociology that from a Christian point of view should not be plugged into biblical theology. God's view on the matter should matter most. If people do not start with God in their viewpoints or discussions, they're not going to stay with you if you discuss these issues from a bibliocentric worldview. God does not want you to leave Him out just because others (sociologists, theorists, professional educators, media) don't bring Him in. Instead, followers of Jesus Christ must address these issues from a theocentric, Christocentric, and bibliocentric kingdom perspective: God, Christ, and Scripture.

There exists great legitimacy in looking at research and identifying problems from a sociological or sociopolitical standpoint in order to gain better awareness of the realities of life such as systemic racism, microaggressions, implicit biases, and the like. But for believers in Christ, the Bible must sit on top of all problems to serve as the defining reference point. If not, our methods, messages, and approaches to rectify racism and its schisms and stains in our land may be not only inept, but may even lead to greater division and furtherance of racism (from both sides).

In bringing us together across racial and ethnic lines, God is creating something new. He is producing the sweet-smelling savor of biblical reconciliation so that the broader society can see His handiwork. One hundred pianos tuned to the same tuning fork will intrinsically be tuned to one another. But it seems like today we've got too many people playing their own keys and their own rhythm with their own cadence, rather than operating under the reconciling rule of God.

Kingdom Race Theology: the reconciled recognition, affirmation, and celebration of the divinely created ethnic differences through which God displays His multifaceted glory and advances His rule in history. God displays His glory through us while His people justly, righteously, and responsibly function in personal and corporate unity under the lordship of Jesus Christ.

This issue of illegitimate division is so critical that the Bible says in Romans 16:17, "Now I urge you, brethren, keep your eye on those who cause dissensions and hindrances contrary to the teaching which you learned, and turn away from them." Keep your eye on those who cause dissensions. Watch out for the dividers. Watch out for language politics that seeks to divide. Watch out for those who post hate-filled verbiage, or condescending statements. Watch for the insulters. The belittlers. Those who judge. Watch out for those in the body who intentionally state or share divisive images or messages on their personal platforms, but then join together on Sunday morning singing about praising God. Division is straight from Satan's playbook. The enemy's number one approach is to stir up division, keeping the body of Christ from impacting the world for God and for good.

John 17:22–24 tells us why this is Satan's strategy where we read Jesus' own words,

> The glory which You have given Me I have given to them, that they may be one, just as We are one; I in them and You in Me, that they may be perfected in unity, so that the world may know that You sent Me, and loved them, even as You have loved Me. Father, I desire that they also, whom You have given Me, be with Me where I am, so that they may see My glory which You have given Me, for You loved Me before the foundation of the world.

The world is not seeing God's glory as it should see God's glory because we are illegitimately divided along racial, class, political, and ideological lines. Those who name the name of Christ still use culture, race, and preference as an excuse not to do the work of reconciliation among each other. Not to talk to each other. Not to listen to each other. Not to read each other's writings if we think they disagree with what we believe. Yet, if we are fighting, marginalizing, dismissing, and downright insulting each other in the global church, the same—and even worse—will be happening in the world.

In the midst of the social chaos swirling all around us, we have been positioned for impact as the church of Jesus Christ. Rather than allowing ourselves to be co-opted by the racial confusion of the culture, we should be operating with a kingdom agenda for race, racism, and reconciliation. Any use of the word *kingdom* that does not recognize and submit to the rule of God based on His self-revelation in Scripture is an abuse of the term. Therefore I am proposing a different, biblically framed paradigm for Christians to use when addressing contemporary racial issues and that is Kingdom Race Theology.

I define Kingdom Race Theology as *the reconciled recognition, affirmation, and celebration of the divinely created ethnic differences through which God displays His multifaceted glory and advances His rule in history. God displays His glory through us while His people justly, righteously, and responsibly function in personal and corporate unity under the lordship of Jesus Christ.*

Kingdom Race Theology sees race, racism, and reconciliation as a kingdom issue and not merely a cultural or social one. As such, it must be first and foremost addressed biblically and theologically if true healing and reconciliation is to occur in the church for the benefit of the society. Biblical reconciliation is *the restoration of a previously broken relationship based on repentance and forgiveness.* It removes the hostility between parties and restores peace and harmony in the relationship. This reconciliation among people is based on the reconciliation God has provided to humanity when Jesus died on the cross for our sins (Rom. 5:10).

biblical reconciliation:

the restoration of a previously broken relationship based on repentance and forgiveness.

This biblical theology of race will examine, critique, analyze, and respond to all social movements against the backdrop of God's inerrant Word. Our theology must inform, affirm, or correct our sociology. Racism in any form must be seen as the humanistic evil expression of the sin of idolatry since it is an attack on the value of the image of God in which all humanity of every race is created. This means that the dignity of every human life must be maintained from the womb to the tomb (James 3:9). Kingdom Race Theology also argues that it is sinful not to recognize and appreciate, without apology, the legitimate distinctives and differences that God has intentionally endowed in the unique racial and cultural makeup of His creation. He is not colorblind as some would argue since He will even extend our racial distinctions into eternity (Rev. 5:9, 7:9). Our identity in Christ is designed to correct and enhance—not limit, cancel, or replace—our racial uniqueness and their usefulness to the kingdom.

From a KRT perspective, Christians should be working together across racial lines to lead the way in repairing the damage done by the long history of racial injustice that affected generational, social, medical, educational, and economic progress. These opportunities were—and in many ways are—limited or denied to people of color, particularly in urban centers. White Christians, and churches in particular, must be willing to come out of the shadows to join with their minority brothers and sisters in identifying and correcting any remaining evils of racism, overt or covert. Biblical reconciliation is always measured by and achieved as we serve together to improve the lives of others. In KRT, unity is obtained through service not just in seminars. It is a theology with solutions, not just a theory about our schisms.

Contemporary social movements should be able to look at the collective work of the church, in our ability to be repairers of the breach, as the most successful and impactful model of how the application of God's kingdom principles can restore the years the locust (of racism) have taken away (Joel 2:25). Rather than siding with, or spending all our time seeking to remove, the movements of the culture, we should be establishing a movement for the culture as Christ's kingdom representatives whose aim it is to influence the culture for God's glory and for humanity's collective good.

However, our illegitimate disunity has muted our voices and stripped our spiritual authority to set God's agenda on race within the context of our land. While biblically and spiritually sound discussions on racial history and issues are strategic, they are not sufficient in and of themselves. Biblical reconciliation is ultimately achieved as we do good works together to improve the lives of people; especially the lives of the poor, oppressed, and disenfranchised. Justice is something we are commanded to do, not merely to discuss (Mic. 6:8).

In KRT, much more time must be given to activating reconciliation strategies than reiterating the problems of racism. All discussions about the sin and evil of racism (which are necessary) and the need for genuine repentance must be quickly followed up with forgiveness and a plan to move forward as one. White guilt must never be utilized as a cudgel to promote a continuous mindset of black victimization or identity as "the oppressed." Forgiveness is key to overcoming a mindset that will keep a person locked in a helpless, inferior state.

Keep in mind, forgiveness never means ignoring the

sin or denying your pain. As Latasha Morrison writes, "Bridge builders don't deny hurt. They experience it. Sit in it. Feel it. But they don't stay in that pain. They don't allow those who've wounded them to control them or constantly drive them back to anger and resentment. Instead, they allow that pain to continually push them into forgiveness."[1] Forgiveness is first and foremost a decision. It is *the decision to no longer credit an offense against an offender with a view to executing personal vengeance.* Unforgiveness is like an untreated injury of the soul. Left to fester, it can set in motion a cycle of events that only harm you more. Unforgiveness can keep you so focused on the pains of the past that you fail to recognize the goodness of God in the present. What's more, when you refuse to forgive, you and God are no longer on the same page.

Rather than siding with any of the conflicting and oft-confusing social and racial movements of the culture, KRT says we should clearly demonstrate on our own how God's approach to racial reconciliation dismantles the oppressor/oppressed distinction (rather than reinforces them) in light of the supremacy of Jesus Christ (Eph. 6:5–9; Col. 3:22–4:1). In Christ we are now to know "no one according to the flesh" (2 Cor. 5:16). This means that divinely created racial and ethnic differences become secondary and reflective of biblical principles and to spiritual and moral Christlike character.

As believers who ascribe to a Kingdom Race Theology, like God we are not colorblind but neither do we allow color to "blind us" from judging people based on who they are and the values they demonstrate through their choices. Character must always come before color. KRT always starts with a framework of personal responsibility, not group identity, since that is where God starts. After all, if racism is the primary cause of all contemporary challenges facing black America, then how do we explain the stability of the black family, the strength of the black church, and the progress and productivity of the black community during slavery and Jim Crow?

We experienced these things as a culture due to the emphasis on values, family, commitment, hard work, and God. As Wilfred Reilly points out, it is the de-emphasis and downright divorce from these values that have contributed to the demise of our culture, as well as the demise of other ethnic or class constructs. He writes, "Empirically, contemporary factor variables such as pay-per-child welfare, no-fault divorce and the normalization of illegitimacy, under-policing of black neighborhoods, and the outsourcing of blue-collar jobs seem primarily responsible for contemporary problems in black communities—and poor white ones. Just maybe, we should focus on and discuss these factors as much as we do the ethnic conflicts of two hundred years ago."[2]

A never-ending conversation of oppressed/oppressor categories in a nation will only exacerbate our divisions, escalating into mere emotional vituperation. It will also support the illegitimate expansion of civil government to resolve the conflict resulting in an increasing loss of personal freedom. We must be honest about what has caused the decline in our culture, holistically. We must also approach social issues without yielding to a victim mindset of them being wholly determinative. There has to be an individual choice to view racism, or its repercussions, as no longer determinative in your life if you are black. You must look at it through a nondeterminative lens. You have personal power through the individual choices you make. Your choices shape your future, irrespective of challenges based on your race. If you don't choose to recognize your own power over your emotions, thoughts, and actions, you risk getting stuck in a hopeless cycle of self-sabotage negating any personal responsibility you have to rise up.

And if you are white, you need to no longer view separatism as saintly. The hope is that you will be motivated to make a difference for God's kingdom through the strategic connection with and working alongside others of a different race. The most effective spiritual movement in the Bible was the church in the book of Acts. One of the significant characteristics of this church was that it was culturally and racially diverse. God did wonders through the coming together of His people who merged strength with strength to impact their culture for Christ.

Kingdom Race Theology insists that our painful racial history should never be ignored, whitewashed, or marginalized since God is a God of truth. People need to know about the 4,500 lynchings that occurred, the destruction of Black Wall Street, and an entire black-populated and successful town of Rosewood, Florida, by racists, the atrocity of slavery, the evil of peonage and criminal leasing. Nor should we reject every aspect of racial social theories just because some of its connections, originations, or conclusions are overtly wrong. We must search for the kernels of truth and apply those to a biblical truth-based common ground. We must also celebrate the achievements of black people in spite of and through adversity. Much more time must be spent on our triumphs and hope for the future than simply rehearsing the pain of the past.

> **biblical love:**
>
> the decision to compassionately, righteously, and responsibly seek the well-being of another person.

However, we must always reject racial conclusions that judge people by their racial identity, positioning them in a perpetual oppressor or oppressed status. This goes against God's Word (2 Cor. 5:16; Col. 3:11; Gal. 3:26–28). We must also reject anything that does not promote or prioritize God's goal of unity through reconciliation. In Kingdom Race Theology, the biblical principle of love must prevail. Biblical love is *the decision to compassionately, righteously, and responsibly seek the well-being of another person*. God makes it clear that this includes loving our enemies while simultaneously condemning or correcting falsehoods and evil actions, yet through a spirit of love, kindness, and dignity.

While we are arguing about ideologies as a culture, those of us who are bibliocentric and kingdom-minded ought to understand, espouse, and live under this unifying Kingdom Race Theology. There exists an alternative that overrules the divisions in our land for those who are kingdom people. When we live according to a Kingdom Race Theology, we will actively seek to overcome the reality of racism and its residual effects with the power of love through biblical reconciliation based on the truth that commands us to impact our culture for good.

FROM GRACE TO RACE

When writing to the church at Ephesus, Paul spends the first half of chapter two talking about the magnificent grace of God. He tells us we are saved by grace, through faith. He also tells us that God wants to manifest His grace in the ages to come (vv. 7–9). It is in this first half of chapter two that we read about our personal calling as "His workmanship, created in Christ Jesus for good works, which God prepared beforehand so that we would walk in them" (v. 10). But just as quickly as Paul finishes talking about grace, he moves to the subject of race. Paul goes from grace to race immediately following the verse on personal and corporate life purposes.

From this flow we can determine a few things, one of which is that a primary "good work" we are to walk in as saved people is the work of racial reconciliation. Experiencing the grace of God in our own lives should lead to seeking to address the injustices and inequities brought about in other people's lives, or our own lives, through issues of race. To put it another way, if a kingdom follower is not about the business of fixing the problems people face due to racism, it is because he or she does not fully understand the glory of God's grace. This grace motivation is at the heart of KRT.

Paul speaks to the racial calamity of his day by urging his readers to prioritize the removal of the plague, or spiritual pandemic, at hand. In Ephesians 2:11–18 he says,

> Therefore remember that formerly you, the Gentiles in the flesh, who are called "Uncircumcision" by the so-called "Circumcision," which is performed in the flesh by human hands—remember that you were at that time separate from Christ, excluded from the commonwealth of Israel, and strangers to the covenants of promise, having no hope and without God in the world. But now in Christ Jesus you who formerly were far off have been brought near by the blood of Christ.
>
> For He Himself is our peace, who made both groups into one and broke down the barrier of the dividing wall, by abolishing in His flesh the enmity,

which is the Law of commandments contained in ordinances, so that in Himself He might make the two into one new man, thus establishing peace, and might reconcile them both in one body to God through the cross, by it having put to death the enmity. And He came and preached peace to you who were far away, and peace to those who were near; for through Him we both have our access in one Spirit to the Father.

Paul calls for an end to racial divisions. Any ideology (or vocal opposition to an ideology) that promotes division is of Satan. Now that they had named the name of Christ, they needed to solve the problem of an illegitimate racial division, in spite of how long it had existed or how deeply embedded its roots had become. Because even though they were on their way to heaven, they hadn't yet learned to get along on earth. It's like the old saying:

To live above with saints we love, oh, that would be glory;
But to dwell below with saints we know, that's a whole different
     story!

Paul was not willing for them to wait to get to heaven to fix this issue of the dividing walls on earth. Part of these dividing walls we erect between us based on race that leads to racism is bringing our histories with us into the present reality. The Gentiles only knew how to be Gentiles, and the Jews only knew how to be Jewish.

And yet they both found themselves sharing the same faith and belonging to the same church. The issues arose when they both sought to bring their pasts with them.

It is important to retain cultural identity and cultural nuances, as well as the knowledge of our historical realities, such as Jesus did when interacting with the woman at the well (John 4:4–9), and Paul did in relating to his Jewish history and heritage (1 Cor. 9:20; Rom. 9:3–5; Phil. 3:5). But we need not impose our racial distinctives to everyone else around us (Rom. 14:1–16). When we seek to do that, we will remain stuck in the confines of our limited views and understandings, and become complicit in causing others to stumble (1 Cor. 8:13; Rom. 8:13–16). This attitude Paul proclaims is a kingdom issue (Rom. 8:17).

This reminds me of the story of the bear who was in a 12-foot square cage at a zoo for the longest of time. That 12x12 space was all he had ever known. One day when the zoo expanded, he was transferred to a 36x36 foot living space. But whenever the bear would walk around, he remained in his self-imposed 12x12 space. That is where he felt comfortable. That is what he knew. He was so ingrained in yesterday that he refused to embrace the expansions of today. He had gotten so used to the confines of the past that he couldn't press on to the future.

And so, it often is when a formally confined minority cultural group seeks to expand more holistically into a majority culture. Established history often restricts each group (both the majority and the minority) to remain apart from the others. It just doesn't feel comfortable to stretch beyond how you were raised, what you were taught, what you expect to experience and more. As a result, we have believers living in racially defined cages, or social media silos, unable to be released into a new environment of intentional integration. It was true back in Paul's day and unfortunately, it remains true today.

One thing I find very interesting in all of this, though, is how easily individuals on sports teams can work together across color and racial lines. In fact, people seem to be able to do drugs together across racial lines as well. Activities somehow manage to pull people together when they are seeking a common goal and yet when it comes to the family of God, all we know to do, it seems, is to split up. I would assert that one reason we so easily split up is that we do not share a common goal—that of advancing God's holistic kingdom agenda on earth. Church, rather, is viewed as simply an extension of our various social lives. And since it is nothing more than an extension of our social lives, it winds up reflecting our social circles—which are far too often racially divided.

But Now

Paul spends an inordinate amount of time in his letter to the church at Ephesus explaining how bad off we were apart from Christ and why we must become one under His rule. He does so in setting up his transition to how things have, or ought to have, changed. We read these transitionary statements where Paul moves from what God did in our lives to how that should affect us:

> "But God . . ." he says in Ephesians 2:4 as he sets the stage.
>
> "But now . . ." he continues in Ephesians 2:13 directing the readers to a better way.

Paul argues that because of what God has done in grace, we ought to be different now about race. Because of grace, we ought to view race and racism differently. In other words, this is a whole new situation. This is a whole new reality. This is a whole new circumstance. And if you do not understand this new thing that God has done through grace, you'll remain trapped in your own racial cage or socially segregated grid. Our problem today is that we have too many Christians trapped in their racial identity who miss the "but now" Christ came to initiate. It's worth reviewing what we saw earlier in Ephesians 2:13–16:

> But now in Christ Jesus you who formerly were far off have been brought near by the blood of Christ. For He Himself is our peace, who made both groups into one and broke down the barrier of the dividing wall, by abolishing in His flesh the enmity, which is the

Law of commandments contained in ordinances, so
that in Himself He might make the two into one new
man, thus establishing peace, and might reconcile
them both in one body to God through the cross, by
it having put to death the enmity.

If you'll recall from the entire passage we looked at
earlier, Paul emphasizes one concept repeatedly. That is:
Peace. Four times he mentions the word *peace*. Racial unity
evokes an atmosphere of peace. Racial division evokes
chaos, hatred, and turmoil. You don't need me to tell you
that. Just read any news article or watch any news program dealing with racial division. It doesn't matter which
side of the debate you watch; you will witness divisive
rhetoric on both these days. Rare is the person speaking a message of common ground, common goals, and
shared solutions. It doesn't matter if the person speaking
claims to be a Christian, division is always a tool of the
enemy, Satan.

Unity ushers in peace.
Disunity flames hearts of pride and hate.

When you and I come to Christ and are born again
as new creations in Christ, we are not tasked with the
primary responsibility of trying to fix something old.
Rather, we are made new. We are now called "one new
man" (Eph. 2:15). This does not refer to losing your

racial identity. What it means is that your racial identity is no longer your ultimate point of reference and identity (Col. 2:11; Gal. 2:20; Rom. 8:7–9).

Kingdom Race Theology argues that racial distinctions must always adjust to our new Christocentric identity when the two are in conflict. When this occurs, the uniqueness of our varied racial and ethnic identities, as bearers of the *imago Dei*, can be fully experienced, appreciated, and manifested for the benefit of others.

Let me say that again because it may sound simple, but the truth is profound to our souls. Paul is not saying that Jews are no longer Jews or Gentiles are no longer Gentiles. In fact, he goes on to talk about Jews and Gentiles throughout all of his letters. Paul did not become colorblind upon salvation. What he is saying is that this new relationship with Jesus Christ as a kingdom disciple is to be the starting point for everything else. It is the reference point for how we are to experience and interact with each other, and even how we are to view ourselves. If you choose not to allow this new identity in Christ to be the glasses through which you view life and make decisions, you will forever live in racial conflict, confusion, debate, and crisis. Why? Because you are starting at the wrong place. Paul says that Jesus, Himself, *is* our peace. He *is* our identity (Gal. 2:20).

Paul is emphatically reminding us here that we are Christian first. Christ is our point of reference. This new point of reference should enhance the uniquenesses of our racial identity, not eradicate them. And, as we saw earlier when examining Galatians 2 more fully, Paul said Christ is our identity right in the middle of a racial conflict. He made this statement in the midst of a racial issue between Peter and the Gentiles. In fact, he went on to emphasize how damaging racism is by saying that Peter's racial "hypocrisy" maligned the good news of the gospel (Gal. 2:13–14). Contrary to what many Christians purport, race and racism *is* a gospel issue, according to the apostle Paul himself.[3]

Jesus is the One who has established a whole new way of operating as believers so that people from different backgrounds can come together in one body, one purpose, and one spirit. When we recognize that our loyalty is to Christ first, and not culture, we discover a new way of relating to one another across racial, class, and ethnic barriers. Jesus wants to reconcile us together through His sacrifice on the cross (Eph. 2:16). He wants to bring harmony, unity, togetherness, and like-mindedness to each of us. Kingdom Race Theology, then, while not ignoring racial history and identity, places its primary focus "the one new man," which then allows us to visibly be the household of God and temple where His Spirit is free to express Himself (Eph. 2:17–22). When this happens, the reality and power of our Christian witness will become clearly manifested before a watching world (John 17:23–24).

When the orchestra is warming up, everything is in

a state of discord. It's just noise. One instrument plays over on the right side. Another one plays scales behind it. Another plays something else entirely off to the left. It's noise. That is until the conductor comes out. When the conductor comes out, he taps the podium. Everyone gets silent. And what was at one point noise becomes a beautiful song.

Now, keep in mind, the instruments aren't the same. There's a violin being played. Or a tuba. Or a piano. All sorts of instruments are represented in the orchestra. And at one point, they all made a lot of noise. But when the conductor calls them together on one accord, they play his song.

What we have today in the church of Jesus Christ are black people playing one song, white people playing another song, Asians playing another and so on. No one can hear each other because we're all making a lot of noise. But in the kingdom of God, we have a conductor. His name is Jesus Christ. Jesus has come, having died on the cross, so that we might play His song. And in this song called "one new man," racism is never to be tolerated.

The cross is not a two-thousand-year-old relic. The cross is a contemporary reality. The cross was established to deal with sin. And racism, in any form, is sin.

Racial reconciliation does not come about by simply stating we need to all get along. That's been our problem. This approach dismisses the reality of the sin that caused the division in the first place. Rather, we must identify the sin, apply the grace of the cross, address the sin through repentance and fruits of repentance so that the reconciling work of Jesus Christ can be ignited. Jesus has the final say-so because He is the foundation upon which all else rests. As Paul continues in his letter to the church of Ephesus, he makes this point clear:

> So then you are no longer strangers and aliens, but you are fellow citizens with the saints, and are of God's household, having been built on the foundation of the apostles and prophets, Christ Jesus Himself being the corner stone, in whom the whole building, being fitted together, is growing into a holy temple in the Lord, in whom you also are being built together into a dwelling of God in the Spirit. (Eph. 2:19–22)

The "cornerstone" was the alignment stone that was used to position all the other stones to it. Everything else depended on the location and strength of this cornerstone. Paul's point couldn't be more clear. If you and I align our thoughts, emotions, and will under Christ and His rule as revealed through the Word of God, everything else will fall into place.

If we are ever going to fix the racism problem in the church for the benefit of our nation, the Bible has to overrule our emotions, thoughts, words, actions, and histories. Our problem is that we have far too many people running to sociology books before searching the Scripture. We have far too many people quoting portions of content from Critical Race Theorists, or *White Fragility, Intellectuals and Race,* or *Shame* before going to the Bible. And while there are legitimate truths present in all of these things, and it is good to read and research various thoughts on the subjects as well as statistical analysis, they must be viewed through the grid of the gospel. They must be seen through the spectacles of Scripture and they must ultimately be made to surrender to the lordship of Jesus Christ.

And every Christian who names the name of Jesus Christ must be actively and purposefully involved in racial reconciliation, according to the Scripture. Not division. Not blame. Not divisive speech. Not dismissiveness. Why? Because unity is what glorifies God and allows His presence to be visibly seen in and through His people. Like a football team, we may come from different backgrounds and ethnicities, but we are to be one team, wearing one uniform. There are different cultures and different backgrounds, but there is only one uniform. We are to head toward the same goal line together, which is the exaltation of Jesus Christ through His reconciled body, advancing God's kingdom agenda on earth through the individual, family, church, and community. This is the goal of KRT.

Only when we get radical believers who take seriously the apostles and prophets as well as the teaching of Jesus

Himself, will we offer a biblical solution to the racism problem in our society. As Colossians 1:21–22 puts it,

> And although you were formerly alienated and hostile in mind, engaged in evil deeds, yet He has now reconciled you in His fleshly body through death, in order to present you before Him holy and blameless and beyond reproach.

If you and I want to see God and His glory made manifest in our culture today, we had better start focusing more intentionally on reconciliation, which is best achieved through ministry together—rather than language and phrases that only further divide us. Christ came to reconcile us to each other and to God. If the church in America had operated according to a Kingdom Race Theology, the last 400+ years of our racial history wouldn't have happened as they have played out. Since Christians have helped to create the racial catastrophe, it is incumbent on us to lead the way in helping to fix it.

It is past time for racism to cease as a dominant force in our land, and in the world, starting with the church. America is not unique to racial and ethnic oppression or inequities. White people are not the only race to have oppressed another race. This is a global sin manifested in racism, tribalism, and ethnic cleansings. It is a worldwide stain on humanity, steeped in historical genocides and racially motivated oppression and, at times, wars.

It is time we begin acknowledging the sin that causes the divide, both nationally and globally and ecclesiastically. This includes acknowledging the privilege (white privilege) that has benefited certain people over others in our own culture of America. We need to acknowledge the collective pain and trauma that resonates in the DNA of generational stigma through inequitable structures. We must confess and repent of the sin of racism. Black people must also confess and repent of the sin of unforgiveness and resentment and the failure to seek the improvement of the level of classism toward other black people who have not had our opportunities to advance.

I understand the cry for "no justice—no peace." But we also must cry out "no forgiveness—no peace." We need both. Both must simultaneously be true for those of us in Christ. Paul's letter to the church at Corinth gives us our mandate on how we are to be ambassadors for unity and spiritual warriors for peace:

> Therefore from now on we recognize no one according to the flesh; even though we have known Christ according to the flesh, yet now we know Him in this way no longer. Therefore if anyone is in Christ, he is a new creature; the old things passed away; behold, new things have come. Now all these things are from God, who reconciled us to Himself through Christ and gave us the ministry

of reconciliation, namely, that God was in Christ reconciling the world to Himself, not counting their trespasses against them, and He has committed to us the word of reconciliation. (2 Cor. 5:16–19)

In short, we are to be "agents of reconciliation." We are not to judge others by their skin or physical humanity. That's the old life. That's old school. That's how Satan and his minions group and target people for destruction. Now that we are in Christ, we are ambassadors of heaven. We are carriers of Christ's views. We are to be about His purpose and ministry, which is reconciliation. Whether that is seeking to help people heal from past wounds or traumas, or even present ones, we are to be about a ministry of empathy, awareness, repentance, impact, change, forgiveness, respect, and grace.

Every Christian who names the name of Jesus Christ must be actively, intentionally involved in reconciliation. We are agents of reconciliation who demonstrate what it looks like when the Word of God has the last word. And when we get radical believers who take seriously the apostles and the prophets and the teachings of Jesus Christ the way we were called and created to do, we will reconcile people vertically to God as we reconcile people horizontally to each other in Christ's name.

It's time for racism to end, especially in the church. It's time to live by 2 Corinthians 5:16 where we are told to no longer recognize anyone according to the flesh.

We are not to judge, stereotype, dismiss, or reject someone because of their race. Rather, we are to live as ambassadors for Christ. An ambassador is someone who
goes to another country on behalf of their country and
represents their country on foreign soil. We are here on
earth to be ambassadors of heaven. Earth is the foreign
country. Our culture is the foreign country. We are here
to show that in heaven, all humanity is reconciled.

There will be a myriad of races and ethnicities in
heaven. God has set up eternity to operate this way. In
the meantime, we are to be about reflecting the culture
of heaven on earth. We are to reflect "thy kingdom come
and thy will be done" on earth. We will be reconciled in
heaven. Love will exist in heaven rather than hate and
prejudice. But our role on earth is to reveal this kingdom
now. We are to give the world a kingdom alternative
that overrides racism, cancels classism, and counter-
mands evil whether it is individual or structural. And we
are to demonstrate what the kingdom of God looks like
when people align themselves on earth underneath His
overarching rule. Adopting a KRT worldview will help
us accomplish this vision.

THE FOCUS OF KINGDOM RACE THEOLOGY

A major focus of Kingdom Race Theology is demonstrating the relationship of biblical justice to the good news of the gospel. Is biblical justice part of the gospel? Or can we do one without the other? White evangelicals have a long and admirable history of evangelizing in black communities, but it sometimes came with an implicit message: Let's win their souls, but not value them as people. It is the lack of clarity in understanding the relationship of the content of the gospel with its scope that opens up the door for the toleration of racial injustice.

We demonstrate a limited view of the scope of the gospel when we ignore, dismiss, marginalize, or degrade the ongoing plight of people in our communities through action, word, or inaction while trying to "save their souls" (Ps. 82:3; Isa. 1:17; Mic. 6:8; Matt. 7:12; Matt. 23:23). KRT teaches that racism is a gospel issue because racism is an affront to the truth that all of us are created in the image of God and, through the salvation of Jesus Christ, become "one new man" in Him. KRT also argues that while the content of the gospel gives the believing sinner forgiveness of sins and the free gift of eternal life, the scope of the gospel seeks to transform the personal life and human relationships as it restores human dignity on earth.

SOCIAL JUSTICE AND BIBLICAL JUSTICE

Social justice has become a convoluted term meaning different things to different people. It is often used as a catchphrase for illegitimate forms of government that promote the redistribution of wealth as well as the collectivistic illegitimate expansion of civil government, which wrongly infringes on the jurisdictions of God's other covenantal institutions (family and church). Such a view of social justice is a contradiction and denial of biblical justice since biblical justice seeks to protect individual liberty while promoting personal responsibility. For example, the biblical injunction of "Thou shalt not steal" includes areas such as government-sanctioned theft through state-enforced redistribution of wealth and illegitimate taxation. When God's guidelines for freedom are compromised then the state seeks to become god, resulting in a corresponding loss of freedom. You then become a slave of the state (1 Sam. 8:9–18).

The term I have chosen to use is *biblical justice* rather than social justice, because biblical justice provides society with a divine frame of reference from which to operate. The word *justice* in Scripture means to prescribe the right way. Since God is just (Deut. 32:4) and is the ultimate lawgiver (James 4:12), His laws and judgments are just

biblical justice:

the equitable and impartial application of the rule of God's moral law in society.

and righteous (Ps. 19:7–9; 111:7–8). They are to be applied without partiality (Lev. 19:15; Num. 15:16; Deut. 1:17) seeing as justice identifies the moral standard by which God measures human conduct (Isa. 26:7–8). It is the government's role, then, to be His instrument of divine justice by impartially establishing, reflecting, and applying His divine standards of justice in society (Deut. 4:7–8; 2 Sam. 8:15; Ps. 72:1–2, 4).

Biblical justice, therefore, is *the equitable and impartial application of the rule of God's moral law in society.* Whether exercising itself through economic, political, social, or criminal justice, the one constant within all four realms is the understanding and application of God's moral law within the social realm.

The cultural disintegration we are now experiencing

comes from a false division of the sacred and secular realms. It was never the Creator's desire to have such a separation exist in His world. From Genesis to Revelation, it is inextricably clear that the spiritual and the social are always to be integrated if life is to be lived the way God intended. In fact, the Bible expressly states that the reason there is social disintegration in the form of all kinds of personal, domestic, urban, and international chaos is that man wrongfully segregates the spiritual from the social (2 Chron. 15:3–6). When God created man, he was given the responsibility to rule the earth under divine authority while simultaneously spreading God's image throughout the world (Gen. 1:26–28). Social justice should simply be the application of biblical justice to the issues and institutions that affect society and its citizens.

However, it was man's refusal to submit to divine authority that led to the first social disintegration. When man disobeyed God, the result was family breakdown, economic struggle, emotional instability, and physical death (Gen. 3:1–19).

When God established Israel, He wrote their constitution in the form of the Ten Commandments. These commandments were divided between man's vertical responsibility to God and his horizontal responsibility to his neighbor. Consequently, God deemed the spiritual and social relationship necessary for the proper functioning of society (Ex. 20:1–17). God also wanted

His people to reflect His character through charitable works and acts of kindness to people outside of Israel as a reflection of their gratitude for His goodness to them (Deut. 10:17–19).

Biblical justice is not a man-made, socially imposed, top-down system ultimately leading to the negation of freedom. Biblical justice promotes freedom through emphasizing accountability, equality, and responsibility in providing a spiritual underpinning in the social realms.

Each of the four jurisdictions in God's kingdom—personal, family, church, and state—is called upon to promote justice and responsibility under God in its own distinct way. Through these jurisdictions, God has given man the task of impartially protecting the "unalienable rights" He has granted to each of us. One way this is done is through the just removal of illegitimate boundaries that prohibit people from pursuing and fully experiencing all that God has created them to be.

biblical freedom: the unimpeded opportunity and responsibility to choose to righteously, justly, and legally pursue one's divinely created destiny.

Biblical justice is not the removal of all boundaries, since boundaries are an essential component of experiencing freedom. For example, a tennis player isn't free to play tennis if there is no baseline. A baseball player isn't free to play baseball if there is no foul line. A fish is not free to roam the jungle, nor is a lion free to live in the ocean. The reason that God allows boundaries is to create the opportunity to take full advantage of freedom. However, biblical justice seeks to remove illegitimate boundaries so that the full expression of freedom can be made manifest. Freedom can be defined as *the unimpeded opportunity and responsibility to choose to righteously, justly, and legally pursue one's divinely created destiny*. Biblical freedom is God's gift to the human race that cannot be truly experienced without functioning within His divinely authorized boundaries (Gen. 2:16–17).

Biblical justice isn't simply a ministry to be relegated to a special event. Biblical justice is a foundational part of fulfilling the purpose of the church as intimated by the heart of God. It is a result of God's people becoming one through being what God has called us to be and participating in what He has called us to do—*justice*.

THE SCOPE OF THE GOSPEL

There is some confusion today about the implications of the gospel, and to what degree the gospel includes this mandate of justice. Some Christians believe that to include social liberation and justice in the gospel is to preach a "different gospel." Others believe that to exclude social liberation and justice as part of the gospel is to deny the gospel. Black liberation theology was formed on this latter thesis.

To resolve this dilemma, KRT makes a distinction between the gospel's content and its scope. This distinction is important because through it is determined the extent that we are to "do justice" as the church as part of our comprehensive responsibility of proclaiming the gospel.

The content of the gospel message is limited, narrow, and contained. Paul made this unmistakably clear when he said,

> Now I make known to you, brethren, the gospel which I preached to you, which also you received, in which also you stand, by which also you are saved, if you hold fast the word which I preached to you, unless you believed in vain. For I delivered to you as of first importance what I also received, that Christ died for our sins according to the Scriptures, and that He was buried, and that He was raised on the third day according to the Scriptures. (1 Cor. 15:1–4)

Clearly, the content of the gospel message is the death, burial, and resurrection of Jesus Christ. Scripture is plain that it is personal faith in the finished work of Christ that brings people the forgiveness of sin, a personal relationship with God, and eternal life (John 5:24; 6:47).

Biblical justice is a foundational part of fulfilling the purpose of the church.

The gospel's scope, however, reaches further into sanctification, within which is located the concepts of justice and social action. We see this scope in Paul's use of the word *gospel* when he informs the Christians in Rome that by the "gospel" they are established (Rom. 16:25). Likewise, in the book of Romans the gospel is called "the power of God for salvation" (1:16) and is said to include "the righteousness of God . . . revealed from faith to faith" (v. 17). This righteousness includes sanctification, since "the righteous man shall live by faith" (Hab. 2:4; Rom. 1:17).

In addition, the gospel is viewed as the criterion of Christian conduct (Phil. 1:27), and believers are viewed as being obedient to the gospel when they are active in the ministry of love to poorer believers (2 Cor. 9:12–13). Paul further exemplified that the gospel involves more than the initial reception of salvation, but also a life of liberty, freedom, and multiracial relationships when he rebuked Peter for drawing evil racial distinctions between Gentiles and Jews on the basis of circumcision. Paul said that in doing so Peter had not been "straightforward about the truth of the gospel" (Gal. 2:14).

The gospel that sanctifies also encompasses the whole man as directly stated by Paul: "Now may the God of peace Himself sanctify you entirely; and may your spirit and soul and body be preserved complete" (1 Thess. 5:23). A view of mankind that divides the invisible world (soul) from the visible world (body) narrows the understanding of the scope of the gospel. This is reflected in a desire to save people's souls, thus compartmentalizing a section of man; that is, to save an aspect of man as opposed to the man himself.

This division between the immaterial and material parts of man leads to a lack of application by way of biblical justice through emphasizing the spiritual over the social. However, the relationship of the soul to the body is to be seen as a unified whole. Biblical terms referring to the spiritual aspects of man support this reference to man's whole person, including the body. The Hebrew word for soul (*nephesh*) refers to the whole person, which includes the body (Gen. 2:7; Lam. 3:24). In the New Testament, the Greek word for soul (*psuche*) is used to refer to Christ's body, seeing as souls do not die and go to the grave (Acts 2:27).

Therefore, KRT argues that the church is commissioned to deliver the content of the gospel (evangelism) so that people can come into a personal relationship with God through faith in Christ. Yet the church is also commissioned to live out the scope of the gospel (sanctification) so that people can realize the full manifestation of it and glorify God. The content of the gospel produces oneness in the church as we evangelize the world together. The scope also produces oneness through good works that are based on the principles of biblical justice and the eradication of racism. When the two are illegitimately separated, you wind up with Christians doing evangelism while simultaneously supporting racist and unjust laws, actions, and perspectives.

Many years ago ago I had the opportunity to sit down with one of the great evangelists of our time, the late Billy Graham, at his home in North Carolina. While we spent the afternoon together, he expressed the concern weighing heavy on his heart. He told me how ministers and churches would work together across racial lines to both plan and implement his crusades; however, after the event was over, these same ministers and churches had little or no relationship with each other at all.

Billy Graham asked me why I thought this was so.

In response, I told him that this happened because the event was only tied to evangelism and not to community transformation as well. When invited, black pastors joined with white pastors to put together an evangelistic outreach. But the heart of African American Christianity hinged on a broader perspective of the scope of the gospel rather than solely on the gospel's content. When asked to participate in community impact and legitimate justice initiatives by their fellow African American pastors, the white church has, as a general rule, often not shown the same enthusiasm of partnership that they receive in their outreach requests.

KRT says that while we must never convolute, conflate, or contaminate the content of the gospel with the scope of the gospel, neither are we to allow the content of the gospel to obscure the necessity for a broader understanding, need, and application of the scope of the gospel. Without a comprehensive understanding of the scope of the gospel, we lack the common goal necessary to bring us together, in oneness, to evoke real and lasting change in our churches so that it can be expanded to our nation.

JESUS AND THE GOSPEL

The greatest illustration of both the content and scope of the gospel is found in Luke chapter 4. This passage took place at a time when the Jews were living in social, political, and economic oppression under Rome. The Jews hated the domination of the Romans, were looking for a messiah to deliver them, and desperately wanted their freedom.

Roaming the hillsides at that time was a man named Barabbas. Barabbas was a leader of a group of counter-revolutionaries known as the zealots. These zealots wreaked havoc along the Judean hills in order to protest and resist Roman imperialism and oppression. Caught in the middle of one of these pillaging raids, Barabbas was eventually arrested and sentenced to death on a cross.

A contemporary of Barabbas was Jesus. Jesus was known at that time as a man of no reputation who had been born in a tiny country town called Bethlehem. While news had begun to spread about Him around the other parts of the country, His greatest claim to fame in His hometown of Nazareth was that He was the son of a carpenter.

One day, Jesus had returned to Nazareth. As was the custom when there was a visitor, He was given the opportunity to read the Scripture and offer the morning's commentary. Having been handed the book of Isaiah, Jesus turned to the place in Isaiah that He wanted to read. We know that He purposefully turned there because Scripture records that He "found the place where it was written . . . " (Luke 4:17). Jesus looked for a particular passage that would deliver a particular truth at a particular time to a particular audience with a particular need. He did so because He had a particular point that He wanted to make. When He found the passage He was looking for, He read,

> The Spirit of the Lord is upon Me, because He anointed Me to preach the gospel to the poor. He has sent Me to proclaim release to the captives, and recovery of sight to the blind, to set free those who are oppressed, to proclaim the favorable year of the Lord. (vv. 18–19)

Then "He closed the book, gave it back to the attendant and sat down; and the eyes of all in the synagogue were fixed on Him. And He began to say to them, 'Today this Scripture has been fulfilled in your hearing'" (vv. 20–21).

Don't overlook that Jesus said, "*Today* this . . . has been fulfilled." The timing of the reading of this passage is crucial. Jesus intentionally chose this passage at a time when the Jews were in the middle of an economic, political, and social crisis. He came on the scene in the midst of a society experiencing the devastating effects of injustice, and said that the Spirit of the Lord was upon Him to proclaim good news: the gospel.

What is essential to note from this passage is that Jesus Himself said that He had good news (the gospel) for those in the economic crisis—*the poor.* He had good news (the gospel) for those in the political crisis—*the captives.* He had good news (the gospel) for those in the social crisis—*the oppressed.* This good news that He had was the gospel of the favorable year of the Lord.

The Day of Atonement

This "favorable year" is called the Jubilee in the Old Testament. To understand it more fully, we need to look at the contextual framework in which it first appeared. We read in Leviticus,

> You shall then sound a ram's horn abroad on the tenth day of the seventh month; on the day of atonement you shall sound a horn all through your land. You shall thus consecrate the fiftieth year and proclaim a release through the land to all its inhabitants. It shall be a jubilee for you. (Lev. 25:9–10)

The year of Jubilee, as noted in this passage, was inaugurated with the Day of Atonement. This was the day set aside to atone for the sins of the nation of Israel both individually and corporately. The Day of Atonement was when Israel got right with God through the shedding of blood—the slaying of a sacrifice. In other words, they didn't get the Jubilee (i.e., God's involvement economically, socially, and politically—an aspect of the scope of the gospel) without first getting their sins addressed by God (a type reflecting the future content of the gospel). They didn't get the social—which included reversing injustice, slavery, family instability, poverty, and oppression (Lev. 25:11–55)—until they had the spiritual. If they skipped the Day of Atonement in order to get the social benefits of the Jubilee, they lost out on the Jubilee altogether because there was a prescribed method for how God instituted His agenda.

A common problem we find in the church today is that we want God to do things for us without the Day of Atonement. A lot of people cry for justice, or for God to pay this, fix that, redeem this, or vindicate that while skipping the very thing that inaugurates God's Jubilee—which is the addressing of personal and corporate sin. God's wrath against sin must always be addressed, which in the dispensation of the church comes through our relationship with Jesus Christ, before He is free to give the social freedom we are looking for. If the spiritual is not foundational, there isn't going to be a Jubilee. KRT seeks to bring the spiritual to the forefront without abandoning or marginalizing the social. This is why the concept of justice is intentionally and intimately connected to righteousness throughout Scripture. They are twin towers that are to never be separated from God's throne comes righteousness and justice (Ps. 89:14). Fathers are to train their children in righteousness and justice (Gen. 18:19). Righteousness is the foundation of justice (Deut. 32:3–4). Thus, the spiritual must never be separated from the social. Biblical justice, then, means doing the right thing in the right way to obtain the right result in the right proportion as God defines it in His Word.

The reason that the Jews didn't receive the freedom that Jesus proclaimed to them was that they rejected Him and His atonement. They wanted the social action without the spiritual interaction. However, Jubilee came as the result of the atonement.

It is important to note that Jesus "proclaimed" the good news of the gospel, just as Lady Liberty proclaims her offer for freedom to anyone who has ears to hear. Lady Liberty does not give freedom to someone coming from Tibet or Burma any more than she does for someone from Kenya. Nor does she force her freedom on anyone who doesn't want it. A person needs to make his way to America and go through the process of applying for and accepting what she has to offer in order to bring her proclamation of freedom out of theory and into reality.

Likewise, Jesus proclaimed good news. He proclaimed the gospel. He proclaimed release for the captives and sight for the blind. He didn't force it by eradicating capitalism and developing a spiritualized socialism. He simply offered it under the condition that it must be accepted through a prescribed atonement before it can be experienced. This is why the biblical church operating on a kingdom agenda worldview through KRT is the only long-term solution to our racial malaise.

Jesus couldn't give Jubilee to the Jews because they refused to deal with their sin and receive Him as their Messiah. Jesus would have provided them with the deliverance from Rome they so greatly desired if they had recognized Him as their future atonement and their Lord. However, the Jews wanted the benefits of the Messiah without the relationship with the Messiah. But that's not how God's justice works. No guarantee of deliverance exists without first addressing the spiritual through the atonement. This is why the church stands poised to be the most effective and most strategic entity in the culture, because it is composed of people who are already living and interacting with the spiritual. Not only that, but since Jesus is the fulfillment of the Jubilee in the church age, and since it is the responsibility of His body to reflect and extend what He has accomplished (Eph. 1:22–23), then it is the responsibility of the church to manifest Jubilee's liberating principle in history. The effectiveness of the church is the key to the well-being of the culture.

Christ as King

Many of the Jews witnessed Jesus feeding thousands and healing the sick, but they demanded that He be crucified in exchange for the release of the rebel leader Barabbas. They chose the revolutionary who was attempting to free them from Roman bondage via a revolution, not the One who would do it via the cross. This is because they only wanted a welfare program rather than to be made well through spiritual transformation. They wanted deliverance, but not the King who delivers. And ever since then, mankind has been trying, and failing, to solve the problems of our societies in like manner, not via the favorable year of the Lord through the Day of Atonement, which is the supremacy of the gospel of Jesus Christ.

There is a direct correlation between the preeminence given to Christ as King and the freedom one experiences. To the degree that Jesus is exalted in personal lives, family lives, churches, and communities is the degree to which the rivers of justice and racial harmony run freely (John 4:1–42).

Jesus' ministry gave the proper order for how to approach all issues of justice and social action. He could have snapped His fingers and delivered all of the poor, the widows, and the oppressed. Instead, He was very particular about His involvement. He became involved in connection with the proclamation of His kingdom message. His purpose was to provide not only physical freedom and relief, but spiritual as well, because He knew that the spiritual and the physical are connected with each other.

KRT insists that Jesus' gospel, as recorded in Luke 4, is the good news that includes both the spiritual and the physical. To make His proclamation merely social is not good news. If a person has the best food to eat, the nicest clothes to wear, and the greatest job at which to work and yet still dies without a relationship with Christ through His atonement, he ends up not having anything at all.

But to make His proclamation merely spiritual is not the full experience of "good news" either. To tell a person that Jesus can give him a home in heaven, but that He can't do anything about where he lives on earth—or to tell him that he's got shoes, I've got shoes, and all of God's children have shoes in heaven, but that we all have to go barefoot on earth isn't all that good of news either.

Jesus' gospel includes both the spiritual and the social. It is designed to build God's kingdom rather than try to save the world's systems. It is designed to provide a model of a different system, one created by God, which provides a divine alternative so that the world can see what God can do in broken humanity. All of the social activity in the world cannot solve the world's problems. In the long term, social action is limited; lasting solutions can only come from the kingdom of God because that's where the atonement guarantees lasting freedom.

Unless social action is based on spiritual discipleship, it will lack the power for long-term transformation.

This is because there is a spiritual reality behind every physical and relational problem. By addressing the underlying theological or spiritual issues, along with the physical, we can achieve long-term solutions because we have addressed the entire problem, not just its physical manifestation. Secular society does not understand the spiritual reality that causes physical, racial, social, political, and economic problems. Therefore, secular society is limited in its ability to impact and transform society.

IMPLEMENTING BIBLICAL JUSTICE

God has a vision. His vision is His kingdom agenda. The kingdom agenda is God's methodology for impacting and transforming the world in which we live. What the body of Christ needs today is to combine our individualized congregations and unite around a fresh view of God's vision carried out in a way that does not negate our own unique distinctiveness. This is why KRT is so critical.

God's vision promises hope both for time and eternity to all who will receive it by connecting the social with the spiritual in a biblically based frame of reference. The social without the spiritual may help people in time but leave them impoverished for eternity. The spiritual without the social may have people looking forward to a great eternity but missing what God wants to do to, through, and for people in history. As we have seen,

both are essential for the transformation of not only individuals, families, and churches, but also our nation.

The church operating on a Kingdom Race Theology
is in the unique position of implementing biblical justice in a country in desperate need of an alternative.
John Perkins declares this boldly: "There is no institution on earth more equipped and capable of bringing
transformation to the cause of the reconciliation than
the Church."[1] But in order to do so, we must pursue reconciliation through a shared pursuit of biblical justice.
We must similarly rally around three key principles for
implementing this biblical justice: restitution, reconciliation, and responsibility. Much can be accomplished
when like-minded kingdom disciples embrace one
another's strengths to work together toward a shared
Kingdom Race Theology vision.

THE PRACTICE OF KINGDOM RACE THEOLOGY

Theology must never be limited to esoteric biblical conclusions void of practical strategies for bringing God's truth to life through our obedience and good works. Kingdom Race Theology seeks to encourage and challenge Christians and churches to lead the way in bringing unity to our land by visibly reflecting it in their lives and through our churches. Since this book has focused on the two dominant racial groups with a shared history of racism in America, I've chosen to include practical steps for both black and white Christians and their churches to take in addressing our disunity. But if you are not in either of these racial groups, you can apply the principles to your own personal life and church in ways you deem best.

WHAT BLACK CHRISTIANS SHOULD DO

1. Appreciate, celebrate, and affirm the uniqueness of our divinely created racial identity, while simultaneously guarding against an unbiblical pride that resists or detours us from biblical truth.
2. Highly value our special collective community dynamic and support righteous movements that seek to correct injustice and promote our corporate well-being. However, we must never allow our group racial identity to erase personal convictions, individual uniqueness, and responsibility. We must never compromise biblical truth and personal integrity for group acceptance.
3. Make the restoration and preservation of the nuclear heterosexual family our highest priority since it is God's foundational institution for a stable, productive, and peaceful community. Fatherlessness and the demise of the nuclear black family is the greatest crisis we face as a people.
4. Reach back to use our gifts, talents, skills, influence, and opportunities to improve the lives of other black people who need the help and hope we have to offer for their spiritual, personal, and professional development. While charity is important, good, and necessary, empowerment is better, and the benefits last much longer. This will create sustainable and strong individuals, families, churches, and communities. Reject all

worldviews and entertainment that belittle, dehumanize, sexualize, victimize, or otherwise demean us as image bearers of God.

5. Resist the temptation to automatically view every questionable action by those of another race as racism. Reject the tendency to stereotype people based on their racial identity, including all whites. Take the time to evaluate the motivation, knowledge, and intent of the person and the deed. Ask questions and seek clarification before making a final judgment. Also, accusations of racism should never be used as a tool to hold white people hostage to white guilt, and thus creating the need for them to prove their innocence as a means of exercising and legitimizing black power.

6. Reject a victim mentality. Victimology nurtures an unfocused strain of resentment rooted in a defeatist identity through which all realities are filtered. Instead, view ourselves as God sees us and with the intrinsic value with which He created us. Even if we have been victimized, we are not victims. We must see ourselves as overcomers. This mindset empowers us with the appropriate mentality to properly address injustices. Where racism is real, however, it must be resisted and corrected. It must no longer be viewed as a substantive impediment to black progress. If our ancestors persevered and made great progress

during the worst of times, we have no excuse today for not maximizing the opportunities of freedom that are at our disposal. Victimhood must be replaced with a *victorhood* mentality.

7. Prioritize spiritual success as we pursue social, political, and economic equality. This will enable us to more quickly overcome the historical disparities that have limited or denied us equal access and opportunity, especially since we often have to work much harder to be viewed and treated as equals. Don't allow money, power, and position to take precedent over our pursuit of a growing intimate relationship with God. We must not automatically and uncritically make the secular cultural standards of success our own.

8. Become an active part of a solid, biblically centered disciple-making church where you use your time, talents, and treasures to advance God's kingdom agenda in the areas of both righteousness and justice.

9. Emphasize as great a focus on personal righteousness as we do on social justice since God holds them in equal balance. Additionally, black leaders and black people should be held accountable for more than our personal, professional, and political commitment and competence in the area of racial justice. They should also be held accountable for the quality of their character. We

must not give black people a pass for bad character and destructive, irresponsible behavior just because we share the same complexion, culture, and social concerns.

10. Do not look to civil government to do for us what God holds us responsible for addressing ourselves, either personally, in our families, in our churches, or in our communities. We must accept, promote, and operate on God's definition regarding the responsibility and limitations of civil government.

11. Educate ourselves about the biblical role and responsibility of civil government and hold it locally and nationally accountable to fulfill that role. This includes civic involvement and voting without simultaneously and uncritically marrying ourselves to a political party.

12. Promote and support a whole-life agenda (womb-to-tomb) since abortion is not only an attack on the image of God in which all mankind has been created, but also contributes to the self-imposed genocide of our race's future.

13. Do not become guilty of the sin of racism or black privilege based on class that we condemn in others. We must pursue God's goal of reconciliation. Perpetual unaddressed anger about racism will drive us to sin and prohibit us from finding a godly solution to the problem.

14. Expand "the Talk" with our children beyond legit-
    imate concerns about police brutality to include
    finishing school, developing strong character,
    hard work, skill development, entrepreneurship,
    the importance of family, and growing in their
    faith. We must never neglect the pain of our past,
    but we must prioritize the achievements in our
    history, opportunities in the present, and the po-
    tential of our future.

WHAT WHITE CHRISTIANS SHOULD DO

1. Accept the fact that racism is a genuine historical and contemporary problem that needs to be
   addressed personally and corporately. Learn and
   grow in your understanding of the history of
   racism and the accompanying pain many African
   Americans and other racial groups have experienced at the hands of white people in general
   and evangelical Christians in particular. Many
   have created scars that still need healing. Such
   exposure will increase empathy while simultaneously decreasing microaggressive behavior.
2. Reject white guilt if you have not committed
   racial sins. White people should not apologize
   or seek to prove their innocence of racism, nor
   should they function with racial guilt for the
   legitimate blessings God has allowed them to

experience, provided that these gifts are humbly, righteously, and responsibly used to bless and not disadvantage others. Conversely, if you find you are guilty of any form of the sin of racism, you should repent, seek forgiveness, and correct the wrong.

3. Recognize how the Bible has been misused and even weaponized as a tool of oppression throughout history. Correct this errant use of Scripture. Bring people into a unified comprehensive kingdom understanding and application of God's revelation on the subjects of racism, injustice, and equality.

4. Support and partner with opportunities for responsible, non-paternalistic black progress, especially for the poor, oppressed, and underserved communities (allyship). This is needed since color alone has never been an impediment for white people in their personal, generational, social, medical, educational, and economic progress—though this had been the case with black people.

5. Understand that many of the generational benefits white people enjoy (i.e., white privilege) are built on the historical forced labor of black people.

6. Expose yourself, family, and friends to diverse racial environments and people who share God's kingdom values as outlined in His Word. Begin dismantling all forms of racism while simultaneously building authentic cross-racial bridges as

God's agents and models of reconciliation.

7. Become an active part of a kingdom-minded discipling church that partners with minority churches to work together on social service and justice issues, especially those issues that can be connected to evangelism and discipleship. Consider becoming an active part of a kingdom-minded, minority-led church.

8. Clearly and publicly reject connecting and marrying your Christian faith to a political party, thus judging and rejecting other Christians who vote differently.

9. Challenge your spiritual leaders to spend as much time specifically addressing justice issues as they do righteousness issues since God holds them in equal balance. Hold spiritual leaders accountable for acts of unrepentant injustice, just as any other unrighteous activity.

10. Expose yourself to recommended black literature, black history, and accomplishments. Visit the National Museum of African American History and Culture in Washington, DC. Discover the voices of black leadership, black theologians, and black ministries that can give you a larger and more comprehensive perspective on the history, experiences, and worldview of black people.

11. Promote and support a whole-life agenda, not just a pro-birth agenda, since humanity is created in

the image of God imbued with inherent significance and dignity from the womb to the tomb. To be created in God's image is to value the dignity of life in all stages of life.

12. Recognize that it isn't enough to *not be racist.* In order to bring about positive changes in our country, you must also be verbally and visibly against all forms of racism (anti-racist), whenever you encounter it on a personal and structural level.

13. Reject the tendency to stereotype people based on their racial identity. Such stereotyping serves to elevate white pride and privilege while simultaneously reducing the dignity and significance of others.

14. Be willing to dialogue with those you disagree with, and read authors who do not share your viewpoints. Engage with documentaries, books, and articles that are outside your normative worldview. Understand that no true intellectual only reads authors with whom he or she agrees. Become truly informed, assess which parts are valuable, then draw your own conclusions. Always allow the Scripture to make the final decision.

After considering what individuals should do, we should also consider what we can do together. Since the church is the primary manifestation of the kingdom and is the primary means by which God is extending His kingdom rule in this world, local churches must be willing to work together across racial, denominational, and class lines. Churches should cooperate in a comprehensive program that connects both the spiritual and social. Churches must work together to extend their influence beyond their individual walls in order to impact the broader communities that they serve.

WHAT CHURCHES SHOULD DO

The crying need today is for churches to become discipleship training centers for developing their members to become kingdom disciples who learn to progressively bring all of life under the lordship of Jesus Christ (Matt. 28:18–20). The church is God's authorized kingdom agency that has been given divine authority (i.e., keys of the kingdom) to exercise kingdom authority on God's behalf in history (Matt. 16:18–19). As such, we are to function as salt and light in society (Matt. 5:13–16) in order to bring divine influence into our cultural reality. Thus, KRT seeks to offer practical things individuals and churches can do to repair the fissures of our racial divide.

For far too long, believers have looked to political, economic, social, and education-based agendas to address the decay now engulfing us. But spiritual success . . . in a spiritual war . . . depends entirely upon spiritual solutions. The kingdom-minded church must accept the responsibility and challenge of leading the way in reversing our racial divide since we, to a large degree, are responsible in helping to create it.

God has given us a three-pronged Kingdom Strategy for Community Transformation for churches to consider adopting and implementing across racial lines in every community.

The decay of our culture is, at its core, a spiritual issue. That is why we believe when the church decides to operate in unity on a kingdom-based agenda that we will usher in true and lasting hope for our land. Churches must come together across class and cultural lines and work toward reconciliation. We must heed the clarion call—from heaven into history and from eternity into time—for Christians to live fully as kingdom disciples.

Unless kingdom-minded influencers significantly enter the discussion and assume the leadership for promoting justice and righteousness in society in order to resolve the division crisis, we will be hopelessly deadlocked in a sea of relativity regarding this issue. This will result in more questions rather than permanent answers. God is not going to bless a country or a culture that comes up with its own rules and asks Him to bless it. God expects kingdom-minded churches to lead the way.

This is a defining moment for us as churches and citizens to decide whether we want to be one nation under God or a divided nation apart from God. If we don't answer that question correctly, and if we don't answer it quickly, we won't be much of a nation at all (2 Chron. 15:3–6; Ps. 33:12). I have proposed a three-point plan for national impact through the church. This plan involves the following three foundational components:

1. *Assemble: Unified Sacred Gathering*
   Kingdom-minded pastors develop a community-wide pastors fellowship that meets regularly and hosts an annual solemn assembly (Isa. 58:1–12; Eph. 2:11–22).

2. *Address: Unified Compassionate Voice*
   Kingdom-minded pastors actively develop disciples who speak out with unified messaging, offering biblical truths and solutions on contemporary cultural issues (John 17:13–23; Matt. 28:16–20).

3. *Act: Unified Social Impact*
   Kingdom-minded pastors collectively mobilize their churches to carry out a visible presence of ongoing good works improving the well-being of underserved communities (Jer. 29:5–7; Matt. 5:13–16).

1. Assemble: Unified Sacred Gathering

Have you ever noticed how special interest groups in our country carry far more weight in influencing our policies and opinions, even though their numbers are but a small fraction of the number of believers in America? They carry so much weight and influence because they unite. We may have the numbers in our favor as an overall body of believers, but we have rarely, if ever, truly united over anything at all. It is time to set our preferences and egos aside and go before the Lord as one body. The problem is not merely our waiting on God to involve Himself in our country's demise, but it is also that God is waiting on us to call on Him collectively, and according to His prescribed manner. I have compiled the following action items (aimed at spiritual leaders) to help us achieve this first point of the three-point plan:

- Start or join a racially and denominationally diverse fellowship of kingdom-minded pastors in your local area.
- Meet regularly with kingdom-minded pastors to strengthen relationships, provide mutual encouragement and to meet the needs of one another.
- Worship together and seek God in prayer.
- Use social and digital media to facilitate communication with your fellow spiritual leaders.

- Train and develop lay leaders who can provide practical assistance and support for meeting your goals.
- Plan and host a local solemn assembly at least once a year, gathering congregations together to seek God on behalf of their community and the nation.
- Share your pulpit on occasion with like-minded pastors across racial, class, and denominational divides.

2. Address: Unified Compassionate Voice

The second point in the three-point plan is to address the issues at hand through a unified compassionate voice. If we could agree to speak in unison on our ideologies and theologies of agreement—rather than spend all our time arguing the portions of disagreement—we would do better at calming the anger and hostilities in our churches and land. In so doing, we could offer several productive yet impactful options for restoration and biblically based equity. A number of special interest groups have been successful in influencing culture because they have managed to unify their collective voice both in the media and entertainment, even though they are small in number. It is time to set our platforms and personal agendas aside when it comes to the matters of national importance so that we can effectively speak into and address the concerns of our day. Here are some steps our spiritual leaders can take in order to do this:

- Seek common ground and shared goals that foster biblical solutions to contemporary issues needing to be addressed, rather than get hung up on the areas of disagreement. Show grace.
- Hold discussion groups and prayer sessions to explore the biblical answers to cultural issues.
- Read and discuss relevant books and videos together to form a basis for common understanding.
- Commit to serving together to work for cultural transformation and biblical values.
- Host community forums to address relevant social issues.
- Collectively meet with civic leaders for relationship building to address issues related to justice and righteousness, and in an effort to influence needed policy reforms.
- Reestablish the biblical importance, permanence, and centrality of marriage and the family as the foundation for a stable and productive society.
- Equip and deploy church members to be kingdom disciples who have transformed lives that visibly transfer the values of the kingdom of God into the societal spheres of politics, education, law, medicine, business, entertainment, etc.
- Utilize the pulpit, platforms, and other ministry opportunities to give an equal emphasis to the issue of justice as is done with righteousness.

3. Act: Unified Social Impact

The third point of the three-point plan is to act together to bring about unified social impact. We will make a bigger impact when we intentionally align our actions with each other in order to produce greater momentum. Here are some action items that can assist ministry and lay leaders:

- Pray for wisdom and guidance as to how you can partner in good works together.
- Work together toward meeting the needs of the local homeless population.
- Coordinate a collective voice in petitions, letter writing, phone calls, and other ways in order to influence political leadership to bring about righteous and just policy and legislative reforms.
- Create an atmosphere where congregants are challenged to pursue relationships promoting racial reconciliation while simultaneously working toward biblical justice.
- Seek ways to collectively address shortages of food, housing, and other basic needs of underserved families in your community.
- Equip and/or shape the mindset of church members with regard to a kingdom perspective as they engage with the culture.
- Build relationships with local law enforcement to foster a stronger relationship and serve as a bridge between the police and the community.

- Construct a network for business leaders who want to assist in creating employment opportunities and economic development for underserved communities.
- Identify key service agencies in your community that you can collectively support in order to facilitate a beneficial kingdom impact.

When we come together to *Assemble, Address,* and *Act* on behalf of God's kingdom in society at large, we will bring about a greater impact as a whole. The scope of our unity will determine the scope of our impact.

APPENDIX:

THE URBAN ALTERNATIVE

The Urban Alternative equips, empowers, and unites Christians to impact *individuals, families, churches,* and *communities* through a thoroughly kingdom agenda worldview. In teaching truth, we seek to transform lives.

The core cause of the problems we face in our personal lives, homes, churches, and societies is a spiritual one; therefore, the only way to address it is spiritually. We've tried a political, social, economic, and even a religious agenda.

It's time for a **kingdom agenda**.

The kingdom agenda can be defined as the visible manifestation of the comprehensive rule of God over every area of life.

The unifying central theme throughout the Bible is the glory of God and the advancement of His kingdom. The conjoining thread from Genesis to Revelation— from beginning to end—is focused on one thing: God's glory through advancing God's kingdom.

When you do not recognize that theme, the Bible becomes disconnected stories that are great for inspiration but seem to be unrelated in purpose and direction. Understanding the role of the kingdom in Scripture increases the relevancy of this several-thousand-year-old text to your day-to-day living, because the kingdom is not only then; it is now.

The absence of the kingdom's influence in our personal lives, family lives, churches, and communities has led to a deterioration in our world of immense proportions:

- People live segmented, compartmentalized lives because they lack God's kingdom worldview.
- Families disintegrate because they exist for their own satisfaction rather than for the kingdom.
- Churches are limited in the scope of their impact because they fail to comprehend that the goal of the church is not the church itself, but the kingdom.
- Communities have nowhere to turn to find real solutions for real people who have real problems because the church has become divided, ingrown, and unable to transform the cultural and political landscape in any relevant way.

The kingdom agenda offers us a way to see and live life with a solid hope by optimizing the solutions of heaven. When God is no longer the final and authoritative standard under which all else falls, order and hope leaves with Him. But the reverse of that is true as well: as long as you have God, you have hope. If God is still in the picture, and as long as His agenda is still on the table, it's not over.

Even if relationships collapse, God will sustain you. Even if finances dwindle, God will keep you. Even if dreams die, God will revive you. As long as God and His rule are still the overarching standard in your life, family, church, and community, there is always hope.

Our world needs the King's agenda. Our churches need the King's agenda. Our families need the King's agenda.

We've put together a three-part plan to direct us to heal the divisions and strive for unity as we move toward the goal of truly being one nation under God. This three-part plan calls us to assemble with others in unity, address the issues that divide us, and to act together for social impact. Following this plan, we will see individuals, families, churches, and communities transformed as we follow God's kingdom agenda in every area of our lives. You can request this plan by emailing info@tonyevans.org or by going online to tonyevans.org.

In many major cities, there is a loop that drivers can take when they want to get somewhere on the other side of the city but don't necessarily want to head straight through downtown. This loop will take you close enough to the city so that you can see its towering buildings and skyline, but not close enough to actually experience it.

This is precisely what we, as a culture, have done with God. We have put Him on the "loop" of our personal, family, church, and community lives. He's close enough to be at hand should we need Him in an emergency, but far enough away that He can't be the center of who we are.

We want God on the "loop," not the King of the Bible who comes downtown into the very heart of our ways. Leaving God on the "loop" brings about dire consequences as we have seen in our own lives and with others. But when we make God, and His rule, the centerpiece of all we think, do, or say, it is then that we will experience Him in the way He longs for us to experience Him.

He wants us to be kingdom people with kingdom minds set on fulfilling His kingdom's purposes. He wants us to pray, as Jesus did, "Not my will, but Thy will be done." Because His is the kingdom, the power, and the glory.

There is only one God, and we are not Him. As King and Creator, God calls the shots. It is only when we align ourselves underneath His comprehensive hand that we will access His full power and authority in all spheres of life: personal, familial, ecclesiastical, and government.

As we learn how to govern ourselves under God, we then transform the institutions of family, church, and society using a biblically based kingdom worldview.

Under Him, we touch heaven and change earth.

To achieve our goal, we use a variety of strategies, approaches, and resources for reaching and equipping as many people as possible.

BROADCAST MEDIA

Millions of individuals experience *The Alternative with Dr. Tony Evans* through the daily radio broadcast playing on nearly **1,400 radio outlets** and in over **130 countries**. The broadcast can also be seen on several television networks and is available online at tonyevans.org. You can also listen or view the daily broadcast by downloading the Tony Evans app for free in the app store. Over 30 million message downloads and streams occur each year.

LEADERSHIP TRAINING

The Tony Evans Training Center facilitates a comprehensive discipleship platform, which provides an educational program that embodies the ministry philosophy of Dr. Tony Evans as expressed through the kingdom agenda. The training courses focus on leadership development and discipleship in the following five tracks:

- Bible and Theology
- Personal Growth

- Family and Relationships
- Church Health and Leadership Development
- Society and Community Impact Strategies

The TETC program includes courses for both local and online students. Furthermore, TETC programming includes course work for nonstudent attendees. Pastors, Christian leaders, and Christian laity, both local and at a distance, can seek out The Kingdom Agenda Certificate for personal, spiritual, and professional development. For more information, visit: TonyEvansTraining.org.

The Kingdom Agenda Pastors provides a *viable network* for *like-minded pastors* who embrace the kingdom agenda philosophy. Pastors have the opportunity to go deeper with Dr. Tony Evans as they are given greater biblical knowledge, practical applications, and resources to impact individuals, families, churches, and communities. KAP welcomes *senior and associate pastors* of all churches. KAP also offers an annual Summit held each year in Dallas with intensive seminars, workshops, and resources. For more information, visit: KAFellowship.org.

Pastors' Wives Ministry, founded by Dr. Lois Evans, provides *counsel, encouragement,* and *spiritual resources* for pastors' wives as they serve with their husbands in the ministry. A primary focus of the ministry is the KAP Summit that offers senior pastors' wives a safe place to *reflect, renew,* and *relax* along with training in personal development, spiritual growth, and care for their emotional and physical well-being. For more information, visit: LoisEvans.org.

KINGDOM COMMUNITY IMPACT

The outreach programs of The Urban Alternative seek to provide positive impact to individuals, churches, families, and communities through a variety of ministries. We see these efforts as necessary to our calling as a ministry and essential to the communities we serve. With training on how to initiate and maintain programs to adopt schools, or provide homeless services, or partner toward unity and justice with local police precincts, which creates a connection between the police and our community, we, as a ministry, live out God's kingdom agenda according to our *Kingdom Strategy for Community Transformation*.

The Kingdom Strategy for Community Transformation is a three-part plan that equips churches have a positive impact on their communities for the kingdom of God. It also provides numerous practical suggestions for how this three-part plan can be implemented in your community, and it serves as a blueprint for unifying churches around the common goal of creating a better world for all of us. For more information, visit: tonyevans.org and click on the link to access the three-point plan.

National Church Adopt-a-School Initiative (NCAASI) prepares churches across the country to impact communities by using *public schools as the primary vehicle for effecting positive social change* in urban youth and families. Leaders of churches, school districts, faith-based organizations and other nonprofit organizations are equipped with the knowledge and tools to *forge partnerships* and build *strong social service delivery systems*. This training is based on the comprehensive church-based community impact strategy conducted by Oak Cliff Bible Fellowship. It addresses such areas as economic development, education, housing, health revitalization, family renewal, and racial reconciliation. We assist churches in tailoring the model to meet specific needs of their communities while simultaneously addressing the spiritual and moral frame of reference. Training events are held annually in the Dallas area at Oak Cliff Bible Fellowship. For more information, visit: ChurchAdoptaSchool.org.

Athlete's Impact (AI) exists as an outreach both into and through the sports arena. Coaches can be the most influential factor in young people's lives, even ahead of their parents. With the growing rise of fatherlessness in our culture, more young people are looking to their coaches for guidance, character development, practical needs, and hope. After coaches on the influencer scale fall athletes. Athletes (whether professional or amateur) influence younger athletes and kids within their spheres of impact. Knowing this, we have made it our aim to equip and train coaches and athletes on how to live out and utilize their God-given roles for the benefit of the kingdom. We aim to do this through our iCoach App as well as resources such as *The Playbook: A Life Strategy Guide for Athletes*. For more information, visit: ICoachApp.org.

Tony Evans Films ushers in positive life change through compelling video-shorts, animation, and feature-length films. We seek to build kingdom disciples through the power of story. We use a variety of platforms for viewer consumption and have over 100,000,000+ digital views. We also merge video-shorts and film with relevant Bible study materials to bring people to the saving knowledge of Jesus Christ and to strengthen the body of Christ worldwide. *Tony Evans Films* released the first feature-length film, *Kingdom Men Rising*, in April 2019 in over 800 theaters nationwide, in partnership with Lifeway Films. The second release, *Journey With Jesus*, is in partnership with RightNow Media.

Resource Development

We are fostering lifelong learning partnerships with the people we serve by providing a variety of published materials. Dr. Evans has published more than 125 unique titles based on over 50 years of preaching whether that is in booklet, book, or Bible study format. He also holds the honor of writing and publishing the first full-Bible commentary and study Bible by an African American, released in 2019. This Bible sits in permanent display as a historic release in the Museum of the Bible in Washington, DC.

See tonyevans.org/krt for video resources including "Tony's Message to Christian Whites," "Tony's Message to Christian Blacks," "What is Systemic Racism," and "Three-Point Plan."

For more information, and a complimentary copy of Dr. Evans's devotional newsletter, call (800) 800–3222 or write TUA at PO Box 4000, Dallas, TX 75208, or visit us online:

www.tonyevans.org

ACKNOWLEDGMENTS

A special thanks to my friends at Moody Publishers for their willingness to publish this strategic manuscript, *and*

To my late wife of nearly fifty years, Lois Evans, for her devotion, patience, and support in the original creation of this legacy work, *and*

Heather Hair for her extensive research, as well as her excellent writing skills and insights in collaborating on both *Oneness Embraced* and this short book.

NOTES

Introduction: Why This Book

1. In *Oneness Embraced* I tell about a 2019 discussion in the Southern Baptist Convention, which wrongly positioned me as fully opposed to Critical Race Theory (without detailing where I see merit in some CRT principles).

Chapter 1: The Need for Kingdom Race Theology

1. Most proponents trace its origins to the killing of Trayvon Martin, and its rise in prominence to the death of Michael Brown.

2. Sony Salzman, "From the Start, Black Lives Matter Has Been about LGBTQ Lives," ABC News, June 21, 2020, https://abcnews.go.com/US/start-black-lives-matter-lgbtq-lives/story?id=71320450.

3. "'We Are Trained Marxists' - Patrisse Cullors, Co-Founder, #BlackLivesMatter," YouTube, June 19, 2020, www.youtube.com/watch?v=HgEUbSzOTZ8.

4. "What Is Critical Race Theory?," UCLA School of Public Affairs, https://spacrs.wordpress.com/what-is-critical-race-theory/: "CRT recognizes that racism is engrained in the fabric and system of the American society. . . . Legal discourse says that the law is neutral and colorblind, however, CRT challenges this legal 'truth' by examining liberalism and meritocracy as a vehicle for self-interest, power, and privilege."

5. Quoted in "What Is Critical Race Theory, and Why Is Everyone Talking about It?," Columbia News, July 1, 2021, https://news.columbia.edu/news/what-critical-race-theory-and-why-everyone-talking-about-it-0. See also the discussion by Ibram X. Kendi, "There Is No Debate over Critical Race Theory," *The Atlantic*, July 9, 2021, https://www.theatlantic.com/ideas/archive/2021/07/opponents-critical-race-theory-are-arguing-themselves/619391/.

6. Leslie M. Harris, "I Helped Fact-Check the 1619 Project. The Times Ignored Me," *Politico*, March 6, 2020, https://www.politico.com/news/magazine/2020/03/06/1619-project-new-york-times-mistake-122248.

7. Robert L. Woodson Sr., ed., *Red, White, and Black: Rescuing American History from Revisionists and Race Hustlers* (New York: Emancipation Books, 2021), v.

8. Thomas Sowell, *Intellectuals and Society* (New York: Basic Books, 2009).

9. Ken Wytsma, *The Myth of Equality: Uncovering the Roots of Injustice and Privilege* (Downers Grove, IL: IVP Books, 2019), 23.

10. Douglas A. Blackmon, *Slavery by Another Name* (New York: Doubleday Anchor, 2008), 57.

11. Ibid., 72.

12. Ibid., 54.

13. Michelle Alexander, *The New Jim Crow: Mass Incarceration in the Age of Color-blindness* (New York: New Press, 2010), 6–7.

14. Chris Pabst, "Baltimore City Schools Graduation Rate Drops to Six-Year Low," foxbaltimore.com, March 31, 2021.

15. Ibid.

16. Thomas Sowell, *Intellectuals and Race* (New York: Basic Books, 2013), 66–67. Sowell cites a Massachusetts Institute of Technology study showing nearly one-fourth of its black students failed to graduate, though they would have thrived at other institutions, due to a system that "turns minority students with all the qualifications for success into artificially induced failures, by mismatching them with the institutions that admit them under lower standards."

17. Heather Long and Andrew Van Dam, "The Black-White Economic Divide Remains as Wide as It Was in 1968," *Washington Post*, June 4, 2020, https://www.washingtonpost.com/business/2020/06/04/economic-divide-black-households/.

18. Shelby Steele, *White Guilt: How Blacks and Whites Together Destroyed the Promise of the Civil Rights Era* (New York: Harper Perennial, 2006), 147–48.

Chapter 2: The Meaning of Kingdom Race Theology

1. Latasha Morrison, *Be the Bridge: Pursuing God's Heart for Racial Reconciliation* (Colorado Springs, CO: Waterbrook Publishing, 2019).

2. Wilfred Reilly, "Slavery Does Not Define the Black American Experience," in Robert L. Woodson Sr., ed., *Red, White, and Black: Rescuing American History from Revisionists and Race Hustlers* (New York: Emancipation Books, 2021), 41.

3. See the discussion on race and the gospel in *Oneness Embraced*, chapter 3: "Biblical Models of Oneness."

Chapter 3: The Focus of Kingdom Race Theology

1. John Perkins, *One Blood: Parting Words to the Church on Race and Love* (Chicago: Moody, 2020), 4.

RECONCILIATION, THE KINGDOM, AND
HOW WE ARE STRONGER TOGETHER

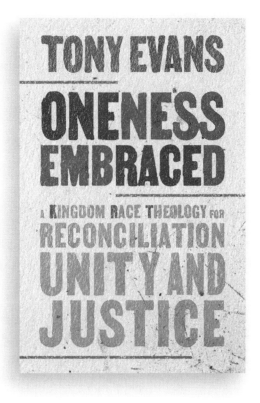

MOODY Publishers®

From the Word to Life®

In this legacy message, Tony Evans seeks to overcome the racial divide and promote a biblical understanding of the kingdom foundation of oneness by detailing why we don't have it, what we need to do to get it, and what it will look like when we live it. To better glorify God and help heal the persistent racial divide, all church members would do well to read and learn from *Oneness Embraced*.

978-0-8024-2472-3 | also available as an eBook

MORE FROM TONY EVANS

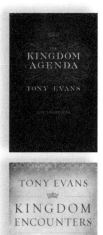

God's kingdom isn't just about theology and church. It is about a whole new way of seeing the world and your place in it. *The Kingdom Agenda* offers a fresh and powerful vision that will help you think differently about your life, your relationships, and your walk with God.

978-0-8024-1061-0

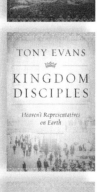

What all Christians need is a kingdom encounter. In *Kingdom Encounters*, Tony Evans explores how the faithful characters of Scripture encountered God—and were forever changed. Join Dr. Evans as he explores how these moments bolster your faith, restore your hope, and make clear to you the face of God.

978-0-8024-1925-5

In *Kingdom Disciples*, Tony Evans outlines a simple, actionable definition of discipleship to help the church fulfill its calling. Readers will learn what a disciple is and cares about, how to be and make disciples, and what impact true discipleship has on the community and world.

978-0-8024-1203-4

There is much God won't do in a Christian's life apart from prayer. In this practical overview, Tony Evans covers a variety of topics about prayer, including its principles, power, and purposes. He will help you see prayer's critical importance and encourage you to make it a dominant mark of your life.

978-0-8024-1484-7

also available as eBooks

MOODY
Publishers®

From the Word to Life®